cakes

100 everyday recipes

First published in 2012
LOVE FOOD is an imprint of Parragon Books Ltd

Parragon
Queen Street House
4 Queen Street
Bath BA1 1HE, UK

www.parragon.com

ISBN: 978-1-4454-6634-7

Printed in China

Produced by Ivy Contract
Cover photography by Mike Cooper
Cover image home economy and food styling by Lincoln Jefferson

Notes for the Reader

This book uses both metric and imperial measurements. Follow the same units of measurement throughout;
do not mix metric and imperial. All spoon measurements are level: teaspoons are assumed to be 5 ml,
and tablespoons are assumed to be 15 ml. Unless otherwise stated, milk is assumed to be full fat
and eggs are medium.

The times given are an approximate guide only. Preparation times differ according to the techniques used
by different people and the cooking times may also vary from those given. Optional ingredients, variations
or serving suggestions have not been included in the calculations.

Recipes using raw or very lightly cooked eggs should be avoided by infants, the elderly, pregnant women,
convalescents and anyone suffering from an illness. Pregnant and breastfeeding women are advised to avoid
eating peanuts and peanut products. Sufferers from nut allergies should be aware that some of the ready-
made ingredients used in the recipes in this book may contain nuts. Always check the packaging before use.

cakes

introduction

There is something about a homemade cake that is truly joyous. The love and care conveyed in baking treats for friends and loved ones; the nostalgic memories of childhood favourites brought to life; the satisfaction of mixing together a bowlful of unpromising ingredients, only for it to be transformed into a heavenly creation. The sheer variety of styles and flavours you can use in cake baking means you can create something delightful for every taste, from chocoholic to fruit fanatic.

Not only is cake baking so satisfying, it is also incredibly easy. None of the recipes in this book require specialist skills or obscure ingredients. In fact, the ease with which you can create a fabulous tasting cake means that involving kids with the baking process can be very rewarding and great fun – and a good way to introduce children to the joy of cooking and creating food. The promise of an icing-covered spoon or mixing bowl to lick will probably tempt any young helper into getting stuck in!

Most of the recipes in this book require only a mixing bowl, wooden spoon, sifter, measuring equipment, wire rack and a couple of cake pans. If you are planning on baking regularly, it's worth investing in cake pans of a few different shapes and sizes, including muffin pans. Both an electric food processor and electric mixer can really cut down the time and effort involved in getting cake mixes and toppings smooth and fluffy. Once you have mastered the basics of cake baking, the beauty is that you can add your own creative flair to the recipes included here – add some chopped nuts to your muffin mix or replace water with lemon juice in your icing, and the recipes listed here can multiply into endless scrumptious variations. From recipes for decadent chocolate gâteaux and fruity tray bakes, to elegant macaroons, you will find inspiration on the following pages to create a great cake to suit any occasion. And after making and sharing a few of the following recipes, you certainly won't find yourself short of friends!

favourites

victoria sponge cake

ingredients

serves 6–8

oil or melted butter,
    for greasing
175 g/6 oz plain flour
1 tbsp baking powder
175 g/6 oz unsalted butter,
    softened
175 g/6 oz golden
    caster sugar
3 eggs, beaten
1 tsp vanilla extract
2 tbsp milk

filling

55 g/2 oz unsalted butter,
    softened
115 g/4 oz icing sugar,
    plus extra for dusting
½ tsp vanilla extract
3 tbsp strawberry jam

method

1 Preheat the oven to 180°C/350°F/Gas Mark 4. Grease two 20-cm/8-inch sandwich cake tins and line the bases with baking paper.

2 Sift the flour and baking powder into a large bowl and add the butter, caster sugar, eggs and vanilla extract. Beat well until the mixture is smooth, then stir in the milk.

3 Divide the mixture between the prepared tins and smooth level. Bake in the preheated oven for 25–30 minutes, or until risen, firm and golden brown. Leave to cool in the tins for 2–3 minutes, then turn out onto a wire rack to finish cooling.

4 For the filling, beat together the butter, icing sugar and vanilla extract until smooth. Spread this mixture on top of one of the cakes and spread the bottom of the other cake with the jam, then sandwich the two together to enclose the filling, pressing down lightly. Sprinkle with icing sugar before serving.

chocolate fudge cake

ingredients

serves 8

oil or melted butter,
    for greasing
55 g/2 oz plain chocolate,
    broken into pieces
2 tbsp milk
175 g/6 oz plain flour
1 tbsp baking powder
175 g/6 oz unsalted butter,
    softened
175 g/6 oz dark muscovado
    sugar
3 eggs, beaten
1 tsp vanilla extract
chocolate curls or grated
    chocolate, to decorate

filling & frosting

100 g/3½ oz plain chocolate,
    broken into pieces
55 g/2 oz unsalted butter,
    softened
175 g/6 oz icing sugar
1 tsp vanilla extract
1 tbsp milk

method

1 Preheat the oven to 180°C/350°F/Gas Mark 4. Grease a
   23-cm/9-inch round cake tin and line with baking paper.

2 Place the chocolate and milk in a small pan and heat
   until melted, without boiling. Remove from the heat.

3 Sift the flour and baking powder into a large bowl and
   add the butter, muscovado sugar, eggs and vanilla
   extract. Beat well until smooth, then stir in the melted
   chocolate mixture, mixing evenly. Spoon the mixture
   into the prepared tin and smooth level. Bake in the
   preheated oven for 50–60 minutes, until firm to the
   touch and just beginning to shrink away from the sides
   of the tin.

4 Leave to cool in the tin for 10 minutes, then turn out
   onto a wire rack to finish cooling. When cold, carefully
   slice the cake horizontally into two layers.

5 For the filling and frosting, melt the chocolate with
   the butter in a small pan over a low heat. Remove from
   the heat and stir in the icing sugar, vanilla extract and
   milk, then beat well until smooth.

6 Sandwich the cake layers together with half the
   chocolate mixture, then spread the remainder on top
   of the cake, swirling with a palette knife. Sprinkle with
   chocolate curls.

grasshopper cake

ingredients

serves 8

250 ml/9 fl oz milk
1 tbsp lemon juice
280 g/10 oz self-raising flour
2 tbsp cocoa powder
1 tsp bicarbonate of soda
100 g/3½ oz butter, softened,
    plus extra for greasing
225 g/8 oz caster sugar
2 large eggs
100 g/3½ oz plain chocolate,
    melted
25 g/1 oz milk chocolate, grated,
    to decorate

frosting

200 g/7 oz unsalted butter,
    softened
250 ml/9 fl oz double cream
400 g/14 oz icing sugar, sifted
1 tsp peppermint extract
few drops of green food colouring

method

1 Preheat the oven to 160°C/325°F/Gas Mark 3. Grease and line a 20-cm/8-inch round deep cake tin.

2 Pour the milk into a jug and add the lemon juice. Leave for 15 minutes. Sift the flour, cocoa powder and bicarbonate of soda into a large bowl. Add the butter, caster sugar and eggs and pour in the milk mixture. Beat with an electric whisk until thoroughly combined. Whisk in the melted chocolate.

3 Spoon the mixture into the prepared tin and smooth the surface. Bake in the preheated oven for about 1¼ hours, or until the cake is risen and a skewer inserted into the centre comes out clean. Cool in the tin then turn out onto a wire rack to cool completely.

4 For the frosting, place the butter in a bowl and beat with an electric whisk until pale and creamy. Beat in two thirds of the cream then gradually beat in the icing sugar. Add the rest of the cream and continue beating until light and fluffy. Stir in the peppermint extract and food colouring to give a pale green colour.

5 Slice the cake horizontally into three equal rounds. Sandwich the rounds together with half the buttercream frosting. Spread the remaining buttercream over the top and sides of the cake. Decorate with the grated chocolate. Slice and serve.

angel food cake

ingredients

serves 10

oil or melted butter,
    for greasing
115 g/4 oz plain flour,
    plus extra for dusting
8 large egg whites
1 tsp cream of tartar
1 tsp almond essence
250 g/9 oz caster sugar

topping
250 g/9 oz summer berries
1 tbsp lemon juice
2 tbsp icing sugar

method

1 Preheat the oven to 160°C/325°F/Gas Mark 3. Brush the inside of a 1.7-litre/3-pint ring tin with oil or melted butter and dust lightly with flour.

2 In a clean, grease-free bowl, whisk the egg whites until they hold soft peaks. Add the cream of tartar and whisk again until the whites are stiff but not dry.

3 Whisk in the almond essence, then add the caster sugar, a tablespoon at a time, whisking hard between each addition. Sift in the flour and fold in lightly and evenly using a large metal spoon.

4 Spoon the mixture into the prepared cake tin and tap on the work surface to remove any large air bubbles. Bake in the preheated oven for 40–45 minutes, or until golden brown and firm to the touch.

5 Run the tip of a small knife around the edge of the cake to loosen from the tin. Leave to cool in the tin for 10 minutes, then turn out the cake onto a wire rack to finish cooling.

6 For the topping, place the berries, lemon juice and icing sugar in a saucepan and heat gently until the icing sugar has dissolved. Spoon on top of the cake. Slice and serve.

boston cream pie

ingredients

serves 10

4 large eggs
115 g/4 oz caster sugar
115 g/4 oz plain flour
40 g/1½ oz butter, melted and
    cooled, plus extra for greasing

filling

2 eggs
55 g/2 oz caster sugar
1 tsp vanilla extract
2 tbsp plain flour
2 tbsp cornflour
300 ml/10 fl oz milk
150 ml/5 fl oz double cream,
    softly whipped

topping

115 g/4 oz plain chocolate, grated
1 tbsp golden syrup
25 g/1 oz unsalted butter
150 ml/5 fl oz double cream

method

1 Preheat the oven to 180°C/350°F/Gas Mark 4. Grease
   and line two 23-cm/9-inch sandwich tins.

2 Place the eggs and sugar in a heatproof bowl set over
   a saucepan of simmering water. Using an electric
   whisk, beat together until the mixture is thick and pale.
   Sift over the flour and fold in gently. Pour the butter
   over the mixture and fold in. Divide the mixture
   between the prepared tins and bake in the preheated
   oven for 20–25 minutes. Cool in the tins for 5 minutes
   then turn out onto a wire rack to cool completely.

3 For the filling, whisk together the eggs, sugar and
   vanilla extract. Blend the flour and cornflour with
   4 tablespoons of the milk, then whisk into the egg
   mixture. Heat the remaining milk until almost boiling
   and pour onto the egg mixture, stirring all the time.
   Return to a low heat, whisking all the time, until smooth
   and thickened. Pour into a bowl and cool, then stir
   in the whipped cream. For the topping, place the
   chocolate, golden syrup and butter in a heatproof bowl.
   Heat the cream until almost boiling then pour over the
   chocolate. Leave for 1 minute, then stir until smooth.

4 To assemble, sandwich the sponges together with the
   filling. Spread the chocolate topping over the cake.
   Cut into slices to serve.

swiss roll

ingredients

serves 8

oil or melted butter,
    for greasing
150 g/5½ oz plain white flour
1½ tsp baking powder
175 g/6 oz unsalted butter,
    softened
175 g/6 oz caster sugar,
    plus extra for sprinkling
3 eggs, beaten
1 tsp vanilla extract
2 tbsp milk
115 g/4 oz raspberry jam,
    warmed

method

1 Preheat the oven to 180°C/350°F/Gas Mark 4. Grease and line a 23 x 33-cm/9 x 13-inch Swiss roll tin with the paper 1 cm/½ inch above the rim. Lay a sheet of baking paper on the work surface and sprinkle with caster sugar.

2 Sift the flour and baking powder into a large bowl and add the butter, sugar, eggs and vanilla extract. Beat well until the mixture is smooth, then beat in the milk.

3 Spoon the mixture into the prepared tin and smooth into the corners with a palette knife. Bake in the preheated oven for 15–20 minutes, or until risen, firm and golden brown.

4 When cooked, turn the sponge out onto the sugared baking paper and spread with the jam. Roll up the sponge firmly from one short side to enclose the jam, using paper around the outside to hold it in place.

5 Lift onto a wire rack to cool, remove the paper and sprinkle with caster sugar. Cut into slices and serve.

variation

To make a roll with buttercream, beat together 115 g/4 oz of icing sugar, 50 g/2 oz butter and 1 tablespoon of milk and spread onto the sponge before the jam.

carrot cake with orange frosting

ingredients

serves 10

oil or melted butter,
  for greasing
175 g/6 oz plain white flour
1 tbsp baking powder
1 tsp ground cinnamon
½ tsp ground ginger
175 g/6 oz unsalted butter,
  softened
175 g/6 oz light muscovado
  sugar
3 eggs, beaten
2 tbsp orange juice
200 g/7 oz carrots, coarsely grated
55 g/2 oz pecan nuts, chopped,
  plus extra pecan halves
  to decorate

frosting

55 g/2 oz full-fat soft cheese
250 g/9 oz icing sugar
finely grated rind of 1 orange
1 tbsp orange juice, plus extra
  if needed

method

1 Preheat the oven to 160°C/325°F/Gas Mark 3. Grease and line a 23-cm/9-inch round deep cake tin.

2 Sift the flour, baking powder, cinnamon and ginger into a bowl and add the butter, muscovado sugar and eggs. Beat well until smooth, then stir in the orange juice, carrots and chopped pecan nuts.

3 Spoon the mixture into the prepared tin and spread the top level. Bake the cake in the preheated oven for 1–1¼ hours, until it is risen, firm and golden brown.

4 Leave to cool in the tin for 10 minutes, then turn out onto a wire rack to finish cooling.

5 For the frosting, place all the ingredients in a bowl and beat until smooth and thick, adding more orange juice if necessary. Spread over the top of the cake and decorate with pecan halves.

coffee & walnut cake

ingredients

serves 8

oil or melted butter,
    for greasing
175 g/6 oz unsalted butter
175 g/6 oz light muscovado
    sugar
3 large eggs, beaten
3 tbsp strong black coffee
175 g/6 oz self-raising flour
1½ tsp baking powder
115 g/4 oz walnut pieces
walnut halves, to decorate

filling & frosting

115 g/4 oz unsalted butter
200 g/7 oz icing sugar
1 tbsp strong black coffee
½ tsp vanilla extract

method

1 Preheat the oven to 180°C/350°F/Gas Mark 4. Grease
   two 20-cm/8-inch sandwich tins and line the bases
   with baking paper.

2 Cream together the butter and muscovado sugar until
   pale and fluffy. Gradually add the eggs, beating well
   after each addition. Beat in the coffee.

3 Sift the flour and baking powder into the mixture, then
   fold in lightly and evenly with a metal spoon. Fold in
   the walnut pieces.

4 Divide the mixture between the prepared cake tins
   and smooth level. Bake in the preheated oven for
   20–25 minutes, or until golden brown and springy
   to the touch. Leave to cool in the tins for 5 minutes,
   then turn out onto a wire rack to finish cooling.

5 For the filling and frosting, beat together the butter,
   icing sugar, coffee and vanilla extract, mixing until
   smooth and creamy.

6 Use about half the mixture to sandwich the cakes
   together, then spread the remaining buttercream
   mixture on top and swirl with a palette knife. Decorate
   with walnut halves.

hummingbird cake

ingredients

serves 10

oil or melted butter,
    for greasing
250 g/9 oz plain flour
250 g/9 oz caster sugar
1 tsp ground cinnamon
1 tsp bicarbonate of soda
3 eggs, beaten
200 ml/7 fl oz sunflower oil
100 g/3½ oz pecan nuts,
    roughly chopped, plus extra
    to decorate
3 ripe bananas (about 375 g/
    13 oz peeled weight),
    mashed
85 g/3 oz canned crushed
    pineapple (drained weight),
    plus 4 tbsp juice from the can

filling & frosting

175 g/6 oz full-fat soft cheese
55 g/2 oz unsalted butter
1 tsp vanilla extract
400 g/14 oz icing sugar

method

1 Preheat the oven to 180°C/350°F/Gas Mark 4. Lightly grease three 23-cm/9-inch sandwich tins and line the bases with baking paper.

2 Sift together the flour, caster sugar, cinnamon and bicarbonate of soda into a large bowl. Add the eggs, oil, pecan nuts, bananas, pineapple and pineapple juice, and stir with a wooden spoon until evenly mixed.

3 Divide the mixture between the prepared tins and smooth level. Bake in the preheated oven for 25–30 minutes, or until golden brown and firm to the touch.

4 Remove the cakes from the oven and leave to cool in the tins for 10 minutes, then turn out onto wire racks to finish cooling.

5 For the filling and frosting, beat together the soft cheese, butter and vanilla extract in a bowl until smooth. Sift in the icing sugar and mix until smooth.

6 Sandwich the cakes together with half of the mixture, spread the remaining frosting over the top, then sprinkle with pecan nuts to decorate.

lemon drizzle cake

ingredients

serves 8

oil or melted butter,
    for greasing
200 g/7 oz plain flour
2 tsp baking powder
200 g/7 oz caster sugar
4 eggs
150 ml/5 fl oz soured cream
grated rind of 1 large lemon
4 tbsp lemon juice
150 ml/5 fl oz sunflower oil

syrup

4 tbsp icing sugar
3 tbsp lemon juice

method

1 Preheat the oven to 180°C/350°F/Gas Mark 4. Lightly grease a 20-cm/8-inch loose-based round cake tin and line the base with baking paper.

2 Sift the flour and baking powder into a mixing bowl and stir in the caster sugar. In a separate bowl, whisk the eggs, soured cream, lemon rind, lemon juice and oil together. Pour the egg mixture into the dry ingredients and mix well until evenly combined.

3 Pour the mixture into the prepared tin and bake in the preheated oven for 45–60 minutes, until risen and golden brown.

4 For the syrup, mix together the icing sugar and lemon juice in a small saucepan. Stir over a low heat until just beginning to bubble and turn syrupy.

5 As soon as the cake comes out of the oven, prick the surface with a fine skewer, then brush the syrup over the top. Leave the cake to cool completely in the tin before turning out and serving.

madeira cake

ingredients

serves 8–10

175 g/6 oz unsalted butter,
    plus extra for greasing
175 g/6 oz caster sugar
finely grated rind of 1 lemon
3 large eggs, beaten
115 g/4 oz plain flour
115 g/4 oz self-raising flour
2–3 tbsp brandy or milk
2 slices of citron peel

method

1 Preheat the oven to 160°C/325°F/Gas Mark 3. Grease and line an 18-cm/7-inch round deep cake tin.

2 Cream together the butter and sugar until pale and fluffy. Add the lemon rind and gradually beat in the eggs. Sift in the flours and fold in evenly, adding enough brandy to make a soft dropping consistency.

3 Spoon the mixture into the prepared tin and smooth the surface. Lay the slices of citron peel on top of the cake.

4 Bake in the preheated oven for 1–1¼ hours, or until well risen, golden brown and springy to the touch.

5 Cool in the tin for 10 minutes, then turn out and cool completely on a wire rack.

variation

To make a lemon poppy seed cake, add half the juice of the lemon and 1–2 tablespoons of poppy seeds before sifting in the flours.

gingerbread

ingredients

serves 9

175 g/6 oz unsalted butter,
plus extra for greasing
150 g/5½ oz dark
muscovado sugar
175 g/6 oz golden syrup
finely grated rind and juice
of 1 small orange
2 large eggs, beaten
225 g/8 oz self-raising flour
100 g/3½ oz plain wholemeal
flour
2 tsp ground ginger
40 g/1½ oz chopped glacé
ginger or stem ginger
pieces of glacé ginger or stem
ginger, to decorate

method

1 Preheat the oven to 180°C/350°F/Gas Mark 4. Grease
a 23-cm/9-inch square deep cake tin and line the base
with non-stick baking paper.

2 Place the butter, sugar and golden syrup in a saucepan
and heat gently, stirring until melted. Remove from
the heat.

3 Beat in the orange rind and juice, eggs, flours and
ground ginger, then beat thoroughly to mix evenly.
Stir in the glacé ginger.

4 Spoon the batter into the prepared tin and bake in the
preheated oven for 40–45 minutes, or until risen and
firm to the touch.

5 Cool in the tin for about 10 minutes, then turn out
and finish cooling on a wire rack. Cut into squares and
decorate with some glacé ginger.

red velvet cake

ingredients

serves 12

225 g/8 oz unsalted butter,
    plus extra for greasing
4 tbsp water
55 g/2 oz cocoa powder
3 eggs
250 ml/9 fl oz buttermilk
2 tsp vanilla extract
2 tbsp red food colouring
    (or 4 tbsp beetroot juice,
    if preferred)
280 g/10 oz plain flour
55 g/2 oz cornflour
1½ tsp baking powder
280 g/10 oz caster sugar

frosting

250 g/9 oz full-fat soft cheese
40 g/1½ oz unsalted butter
3 tbsp caster sugar
1 tsp vanilla extract

method

1 Preheat the oven to 190°C/375°F/Gas Mark 5. Grease two 23-cm/9-inch sandwich tins and line the bases with baking paper.

2 Place the butter, water and cocoa powder in a small saucepan and heat gently, without boiling, stirring until melted and smooth. Remove from the heat and leave to cool slightly.

3 Beat together the eggs, buttermilk, vanilla extract and food colouring until frothy. Beat in the butter mixture. Sift together the flour, cornflour and baking powder, then stir quickly and evenly into the egg mixture with the caster sugar.

4 Divide the mixture between the prepared tins and bake in the preheated oven for 25–30 minutes, or until risen and firm to the touch. Leave to cool in the tins for 3–4 minutes, then turn out and finish cooling on a wire rack.

5 For the frosting, beat together all the ingredients until smooth. Use about half of the frosting to sandwich the cakes together, then spread the remainder over the top, swirling with a palette knife.

rich fruit cake

ingredients

serves 16

350 g/12 oz sultanas

225 g/8 oz raisins

115 g/4 oz ready-to-eat dried apricots, chopped

85 g/3 oz stoned dates, chopped

4 tbsp dark rum or brandy, plus extra for flavouring (optional)

finely grated rind and juice of 1 orange

oil or melted butter, for greasing

225 g/8 oz unsalted butter

225 g/8 oz light muscovado sugar

4 eggs, beaten

70 g/2½ oz chopped mixed peel

85 g/3 oz glacé cherries, quartered

25 g/1 oz chopped glacé ginger or stem ginger

40 g/1½ oz blanched almonds, chopped

200 g/7 oz plain flour

1 tsp ground mixed spice

method

1 Place the sultanas, raisins, apricots and dates in a large bowl and stir in the rum, orange rind and orange juice. Cover and leave to soak for several hours or overnight.

2 Preheat the oven to 150°C/300°F/Gas Mark 2. Grease a 20-cm/8-inch round deep cake tin and line with baking paper.

3 Cream together the butter and sugar until light and fluffy. Gradually beat in the eggs, beating hard after each addition. Stir in the soaked fruits, mixed peel, glacé cherries, glacé ginger and blanched almonds.

4 Sift together the flour and mixed spice, then fold lightly and evenly into the mixture. Spoon the mixture into the prepared cake tin and level the surface, making a slight depression in the centre with the back of the spoon.

5 Bake in the preheated oven for 2¼–2¾ hours, or until the cake is beginning to shrink away from the sides and a skewer inserted into the centre comes out clean. Cool completely in the tin.

6 Turn out the cake and remove the lining paper. Wrap in greaseproof paper and foil, and store for at least two months before use. To add a richer flavour, prick the cake with a skewer and spoon over a couple of extra tablespoons of rum or brandy, if using, before storing.

classic cherry cake

ingredients

serves 6

oil or melted butter,
    for greasing
250 g/9 oz glacé cherries,
    quartered
85 g/3 oz ground almonds
200 g/7 oz plain flour
1 tsp baking powder
200 g/7 oz unsalted butter
200 g/7 oz caster sugar
3 large eggs
finely grated rind and
    juice of 1 lemon
6 sugar cubes, crushed

method

1 Preheat the oven to 180°C/350°F/Gas Mark 4. Grease a 20-cm/8-inch round cake tin and line with baking paper.

2 Stir together the cherries, ground almonds and 1 tablespoon of the flour. Sift the remaining flour into a separate bowl with the baking powder.

3 Cream together the butter and caster sugar until light in colour and fluffy in texture. Gradually add the eggs, beating hard with each addition, until evenly mixed.

4 Add the flour mixture and fold lightly and evenly into the creamed mixture with a metal spoon. Add the cherry mixture and fold in evenly. Finally, fold in the lemon rind and juice.

5 Spoon the mixture into the prepared cake tin and sprinkle with the crushed sugar cubes. Bake in the preheated oven for 1–1¼ hours, or until risen, golden brown and the cake is just beginning to shrink away from the sides of the tin.

6 Leave to cool in the tin for 15 minutes, then turn out onto a wire rack to finish cooling.

battenberg cake

ingredients

serves 6–8

115 g/4 oz butter or margarine,
  softened, plus extra for
  greasing
115 g/4 oz caster sugar,
  plus extra for sprinkling
2 eggs, lightly beaten
1 tsp vanilla extract
115 g/4 oz self-raising flour,
  sifted
a few drops of pink food
  colouring
2–3 tbsp apricot jam
300 g/10½ oz marzipan

method

1 Preheat the oven to 180°C/350°F/Gas Mark 4. Grease and line an 18-cm/7-inch shallow square baking tin. Cut a strip of double baking paper and grease it. Use this to divide the tin in half.

2 Cream the butter and sugar in a mixing bowl until pale and fluffy. Gently beat in the eggs and vanilla extract, and add the flour. Spoon half the mixture into a separate bowl and add a few drops of food colouring. Spoon the plain mixture into half the prepared baking tin. Spoon the coloured mixture into the other half of the tin. Bake in the preheated oven for 35–40 minutes. Turn out and leave to cool on a wire rack.

3 When cool, trim the edges and cut the cake portions lengthways in half, making four equal parts. Warm the jam in a small saucepan. Brush two sides of each cake portion with some of the jam and stick them together to give a chequerboard effect. Knead the marzipan with a few drops of pink food colouring. Roll out the marzipan to a rectangle wide enough to wrap around the cake. Brush the outside of the cake with the remaining jam. Place the cake on the marzipan and wrap around the cake, making sure that the seam is on one corner of the cake. Trim the edges neatly. Crimp the top edges of the cake, if desired, and sprinkle with sugar.

cupcakes, muffins & bars

vanilla frosted cupcakes

ingredients

makes 12

115 g/4 oz unsalted butter, softened
115 g/4 oz golden caster sugar
2 eggs, lightly beaten
115 g/4 oz self-raising flour
1 tbsp milk
crystallized rose petals, to decorate

frosting

175 g/6 oz unsalted butter, softened
2 tsp vanilla extract
2 tbsp milk
300 g/10½ oz icing sugar, sifted

method

1 Preheat the oven to 180°C/350°F/Gas Mark 4. Put 12 paper baking cases in a muffin tin.

2 Place the butter and sugar in a bowl and beat together until light and fluffy. Gradually beat in the eggs. Sift in the flour and fold in gently using a metal spoon. Fold in the milk.

3 Spoon the mixture into the paper cases. Bake in the preheated oven for 15–20 minutes until golden brown and firm to the touch. Transfer to a wire rack and leave to cool.

4 For the frosting, put the butter, vanilla extract and milk in a large bowl. Using an electric whisk, beat the mixture until smooth. Gradually beat in the icing sugar and continue beating for 2–3 minutes until the frosting is very light and creamy.

5 Spoon the frosting into a large piping bag fitted with a large star nozzle and pipe swirls of the frosting onto the top of each cupcake. Decorate each cupcake with crystallized rose petals.

raspberry ripple cupcakes

ingredients

makes 32

175 g/6 oz plain white flour
1 tbsp baking powder
1 tbsp cornflour
175 g/6 oz unsalted butter, softened
175 g/6 oz caster sugar
3 eggs, beaten
1 tsp almond essence
200 g/7 oz fresh raspberries
vanilla sugar, for sprinkling

method

1 Preheat the oven to 190°C/375°F/Gas Mark 5. Put 32 paper baking cases into bun tins or put 32 double-layer paper cases onto baking trays.

2 Sift the flour, baking powder and cornflour into a large bowl and add the butter, caster sugar, eggs and almond essence. Beat well until the mixture is smooth. Mash the raspberries lightly with a fork, then fold into the mixture.

3 Divide the mixture between the paper cases. Bake in the preheated oven for 15–20 minutes, or until risen, firm and golden brown.

4 Transfer the cupcakes to a wire rack to cool. Sprinkle with vanilla sugar before serving.

chewy flapjack cupcakes

ingredients

makes 8

55 g/2 oz butter, softened
55 g/2 oz golden caster sugar
1 large egg, lightly beaten
55 g/2 oz self-raising flour

topping

40 g/1½ oz soft margarine
40 g/1½ oz demerara sugar
1 tbsp golden syrup
55 g/2 oz rolled oats

method

1 Preheat the oven to 190°C/375°F/Gas Mark 5. Put 8 paper baking cases in a bun tin or put 8 double-layer paper cases on a baking tray.

2 For the flapjack topping, place the margarine, demerara sugar and golden syrup in a small saucepan and heat gently until the margarine has melted. Stir in the oats. Set aside.

3 Put the butter and sugar in a bowl and beat together until light and fluffy. Gradually beat in the egg. Sift in the flour and, using a metal spoon, fold gently into the mixture. Spoon the mixture into the paper cases. Gently spoon the flapjack topping over the top.

4 Bake in the preheated oven for 20 minutes, or until well risen and the topping is golden brown. Transfer to a wire rack to cool completely.

pistachio cupcakes
with tangy lime frosting

ingredients

makes 16

85 g/3 oz unsalted pistachio nuts
115 g/4 oz butter, softened
140 g/5 oz golden caster sugar
140 g/5 oz self-raising flour
2 eggs, lightly beaten
4 tbsp Greek-style yogurt
1 tbsp chopped pistachio nuts

frosting

115 g/4 oz butter, softened
2 tbsp lime juice cordial
few drops of green food colouring
    (optional)
200 g/7 oz icing sugar

method

1 Preheat the oven to 180°C/350°F/Gas Mark 4. Put 16 paper baking cases in bun tins or 16 double-layer paper cases on a baking tray.

2 Put the pistachio nuts in a food processor or blender and process for a few seconds until finely ground. Add the butter, sugar, flour, eggs and yogurt and then process until evenly mixed. Spoon the mixture into the paper cases.

3 Bake the cupcakes in the preheated oven for 20–25 minutes, or until well risen and springy to the touch. Transfer to a wire rack and leave to cool completely.

4 For the frosting, put the butter, lime cordial and food colouring, if using, in a bowl and beat until light and fluffy. Sift in the icing sugar and beat until smooth. Swirl the frosting over each cupcake and sprinkle with the chopped pistachio nuts.

maple pecan cupcakes

ingredients

makes 30

175 g/6 oz plain white flour
1 tbsp baking powder
175 g/6 oz unsalted butter,
    softened
115 g/4 oz light muscovado
    sugar
4 tbsp maple syrup
3 eggs, beaten
1 tsp vanilla extract
30 g/1 oz pecan nuts,
    finely chopped

topping

40 g/1½ oz pecan nuts,
    finely chopped
2 tbsp plain white flour
2 tbsp light muscovado sugar
2 tbsp melted butter

method

1 Preheat the oven to 190°C/375°F/Gas Mark 5. Put 30 paper baking cases into bun tins or put 30 double-laye paper cases onto baking trays.

2 Sift the flour and baking powder into a large bowl and add the butter, sugar, maple syrup, eggs and vanilla extract. Beat well until the mixture is smooth, then stir in the pecan nuts.

3 Divide the mixture between the paper cases. For the topping, mix together the pecans, flour, sugar and melted butter to make a crumbly mixture and spoon a little on top of each cupcake.

4 Bake in the preheated oven for 15–20 minutes, or until risen, firm and golden brown. Transfer the cupcakes to a wire rack to cool.

honey & spice cupcakes

ingredients

makes 22–24

140 g/5 oz unsalted butter
100 g/3½ oz light muscovado sugar
100 g/3½ oz honey
200 g/7 oz self-raising flour
1 tsp ground allspice
2 eggs, beaten
22–24 whole blanched almonds

method

1 Preheat the oven to 180°C/350°F/Gas Mark 4. Put 22–24 paper baking cases into shallow bun tins.

2 Place the butter, sugar and honey in a large saucepan and heat gently, stirring, until the butter is melted. Remove the pan from the heat.

3 Sift together the flour and allspice and stir into the mixture in the saucepan, then beat in the eggs, mixing to a smooth batter.

4 Spoon the mixture into the paper cases and place an almond on top of each one. Bake in the preheated oven for 20–25 minutes, or until well risen and golden brown. Transfer to a wire rack to cool.

rocky road cupcakes

ingredients

makes 12

2 tbsp cocoa powder
2 tbsp hot water
115 g/4 oz butter, softened
115 g/4 oz caster sugar
2 eggs, lightly beaten
115 g/4 oz self-raising flour

topping

25 g/1 oz chopped mixed nuts
100 g/3½ oz milk chocolate, melted
115 g/4 oz mini marshmallows
40 g/1½ oz glacé cherries, chopped

method

1 Preheat the oven to 180°C/350°F/Gas Mark 4. Put 12 paper muffin cases in a muffin tin or put 12 double-layer paper cases on a baking tray.

2 Blend the cocoa powder and hot water together and set aside. Put the butter and sugar in a bowl and beat together until light and fluffy. Gradually beat in the eggs, then beat in the blended cocoa. Sift in the flour and, using a metal spoon, fold gently into the mixture. Spoon the mixture into the paper cases.

3 Bake in the preheated oven for 20 minutes, or until well risen and springy to the touch. Transfer to a wire rack to cool completely.

4 For the topping, stir the nuts into the melted chocolate and spread a little of the mixture over the top of the cakes. Lightly stir the marshmallows and cherries into the remaining chocolate mixture and pile on top of the cupcakes. Leave to set.

chocolate & orange cupcakes

ingredients

makes 16

115 g/4 oz butter, softened
115 g/4 oz golden caster sugar
finely grated rind and juice
    of ½ orange
2 eggs, lightly beaten
115 g/4 oz self-raising flour
25 g/1 oz plain chocolate, grated
thin strips candied orange peel,
    to decorate

topping

115 g/4 oz plain chocolate,
    broken into pieces
25 g/1 oz unsalted butter
1 tbsp golden syrup

method

1 Preheat the oven to 180°C/350°F/Gas Mark 4.
   Put 16 paper baking cases in bun tins or put 16
   double-layer paper cases on a baking tray.

2 Put the butter, sugar and orange rind in a bowl and
   beat together until light and fluffy. Gradually beat in
   the eggs. Sift in the flour and, using a metal spoon,
   fold gently into the mixture with the orange juice
   and grated chocolate. Spoon the cake mixture into
   the paper cases.

3 Bake the cupcakes in the preheated oven for
   20 minutes, or until well risen and springy to the
   touch. Transfer to a wire rack to cool completely.

4 For the topping, put the chocolate into a heatproof
   bowl and add the butter and syrup. Set the bowl over
   a saucepan of gently simmering water and heat until
   melted. Remove from the heat and stir until smooth.
   Cool until the topping is thick enough to spread.
   Spread over the cupcakes and decorate each cupcake
   with a few strips of candied orange peel. Leave to set.

coffee fudge cupcakes

ingredients

makes 28

175 g/6 oz plain white flour
1 tbsp baking powder
175 g/6 oz unsalted butter, softened
175 g/6 oz caster sugar
3 eggs, beaten
1 tsp coffee extract
2 tbsp milk
chocolate-covered coffee beans, to decorate

frosting

55 g/2 oz unsalted butter
115 g/4 oz light muscovado sugar
2 tbsp single cream or milk
½ tsp coffee extract
400 g/14 oz icing sugar, sifted

method

1 Preheat the oven to 190°C/375°F/Gas Mark 5. Put 28 paper cases into bun tins or put 28 double-layer paper cases onto baking trays.

2 Sift the flour and baking powder into a large bowl and add the butter, caster sugar, eggs and coffee extract. Beat well until the mixture is smooth, then beat in the milk.

3 Divide the mixture between the paper cases. Bake in the preheated oven for 15–20 minutes, or until risen, firm and golden brown. Transfer the cupcakes to a wire rack to cool.

4 For the frosting, place the butter, muscovado sugar, cream and coffee extract in a saucepan over a medium heat and stir until melted and smooth. Bring to the boil and boil, stirring, for 2 minutes. Remove from the heat and beat in the icing sugar.

5 Stir the frosting until smooth and thick, then spoon into a piping bag fitted with a large star nozzle. Pipe a swirl of frosting on top of each cupcake and top with a coffee bean.

butterscotch cupcakes

ingredients

makes 28

175 g/6 oz plain white flour
1 tbsp baking powder
175 g/6 oz unsalted butter, softened
175 g/6 oz light muscovado sugar
3 eggs, beaten
1 tsp vanilla extract

topping

2 tbsp golden syrup
25 g/1 oz unsalted butter
2 tbsp light muscovado sugar

method

1 Preheat the oven to 190°C/375°F/Gas Mark 5. Put 28 paper cases into bun tins or put 28 double-layer paper cases onto baking trays.

2 Sift the flour and baking powder into a large bowl and add the butter, sugar, eggs and vanilla extract. Beat well until the mixture is smooth.

3 Divide the mixture between the paper cases. Bake in the preheated oven for 15–20 minutes, or until risen, firm and golden brown. Transfer the cupcakes to a wire rack to cool.

4 For the topping, place the golden syrup, butter and sugar in a small pan and heat gently, stirring, until the sugar dissolves. Bring to the boil and cook, stirring, for about 1 minute. Drizzle over the cupcakes and leave to set.

blueberry & vanilla muffins

ingredients
makes 18

125 g/4½ oz self-raising flour
½ tsp baking powder
70 g/2½ oz caster sugar
85 g/3 oz blueberries
2 tsp vanilla extract
1 egg
125 ml/4 fl oz buttermilk
2 tbsp vegetable oil
vanilla sugar, for dusting

method

1 Preheat the oven to 190°C/375°F/Gas Mark 5. Cut out 18 x 9-cm/3½-inch squares from baking paper. Push the squares into 2 x 12-hole mini muffin tins, creasing the squares to fit so that they form paper cases. Don't worry if they lift out of the sections slightly; the weight of the muffin mixture will hold them in place.

2 Sift the flour and baking powder into a mixing bowl. Stir in the sugar and blueberries. In a separate mixing bowl, beat together the vanilla, egg, buttermilk and oil with a fork until evenly combined.

3 Tip the buttermilk mixture into the flour. Using a dessertspoon, gently fold the ingredients together until only just mixed. Don't over-blend the ingredients or the muffins won't be as light.

4 Spoon the mixture into the paper cases; it should be level with the top of the tin. Sprinkle with a little vanilla sugar and bake in the preheated oven for 15 minutes, or until risen and just firm to the touch. Leave the muffins in the tin for 2 minutes, then transfer them in their cases to a wire rack to cool. Serve warm or cold, dusted with extra vanilla sugar.

double chocolate brownies

ingredients

makes 9

115 g/4 oz butter, plus extra
for greasing
115 g/4 oz plain chocolate,
broken into pieces
300 g/10½ oz golden
caster sugar
pinch of salt
1 tsp vanilla extract
2 large eggs
140 g/5 oz plain flour
2 tbsp cocoa powder
100 g/3½ oz white
chocolate chips

sauce

50 g/2 oz butter
225 g/8 oz golden caster sugar
150 ml/5 fl oz milk
250 ml/9 fl oz double cream
225 g/8 oz golden syrup
200 g/7 oz plain chocolate,
broken into pieces

method

1 Preheat the oven to 180°C/350°F/Gas Mark 4. Grease an 18-cm/7-inch square cake tin and line the base with baking paper.

2 Place the butter and chocolate in a small heatproof bowl set over a saucepan of gently simmering water until melted. Stir until smooth. Leave to cool slightly. Stir in the sugar, salt and vanilla extract. Add the eggs, one at a time, and stir until blended.

3 Sift the flour and cocoa powder into the mixture and beat until smooth. Stir in the chocolate chips, then pour the mixture into the prepared tin. Bake in the preheated oven for 35–40 minutes, or until the top is evenly coloured and a cocktail stick inserted into the centre comes out almost clean. Leave to cool slightly while you prepare the sauce.

4 For the fudge sauce, place the butter, sugar, milk, cream and golden syrup in a small saucepan and heat gently until the sugar has dissolved. Bring to the boil and stir for 10 minutes, or until the mixture is caramel coloured. Remove from the heat and add the chocolate. Stir until smooth. Cut the brownies into squares and serve immediately with the sauce.

vanilla swirled brownies

ingredients

makes 12

85 g/3 oz lightly salted butter,
   plus extra for greasing
100 g/3½ oz plain chocolate,
   roughly chopped
1 egg
1 egg yolk
100 g/3½ oz light muscovado
   sugar
40 g/1½ oz self-raising flour
¼ tsp baking powder
85 g/3 oz milk chocolate,
   roughly chopped

frosting

150 g/5½ oz mascarpone cheese
4 tbsp icing sugar
1 tsp vanilla extract
milk or plain chocolate curls,
   to sprinkle

method

1 Preheat the oven to 190°C/375°F/Gas Mark 5. Grease and base-line a 12-hole mini muffin tin.

2 Put the butter and plain chocolate in a heatproof bowl, set the bowl over a saucepan of gently simmering water and heat until melted. Leave the mixture to cool slightly.

3 Put the egg, egg yolk and light muscovado sugar in a mixing bowl and beat together with an electric whisk until the mixture begins to turn frothy. Stir in the melted chocolate. Sift the flour and baking powder into the bowl, scatter in the milk chocolate and stir together. Using a teaspoon, spoon the mixture into the muffin tin.

4 Bake in the preheated oven for 12–15 minutes, or until the crust feels dry but gives a little when gently pressed. Leave in the tin for 10 minutes, then transfer to a wire rack to cool.

5 For the frosting, put the mascarpone cheese, icing sugar and vanilla in a small bowl and beat with an electric whisk until smooth and creamy. Put the mixture in a piping bag fitted with a 1-cm/½-inch star nozzle and pipe swirls over the cakes. Sprinkle with chocolate curls.

marshmallow crunch bars

ingredients

makes 8

oil or melted butter,
    for greasing
175 g/6 oz plain white flour
1 tbsp baking powder
175 g/6 oz unsalted butter,
    softened
175 g/6 oz caster sugar
3 eggs, beaten
1 tsp vanilla extract
100 g/3½ oz chopped
    mixed nuts
85 g/3 oz glacé cherries,
    roughly chopped
55 g/2 oz mini marshmallows

method

1 Preheat the oven to 180°C/350°F/Gas Mark 4. Grease and line a 23-cm/9-inch square cake tin.

2 Sift the flour and baking powder into a large bowl and add the butter, sugar, eggs and vanilla extract. Beat well until the mixture is smooth. Stir about two thirds of the nuts and glacé cherries into the mixture.

3 Spoon the mixture into the prepared tin and smooth level with a palette knife. Scatter the remaining nuts and glacé cherries and the marshmallows over the top, pressing down lightly.

4 Bake in the preheated oven for 40–50 minutes, or until risen and golden brown.

5 Leave to cool in the tin for about 20 minutes, until firm, then cut into bars and finish cooling on a wire rack.

hazelnut bars

ingredients

makes 16

150 g/5½ oz plain flour
pinch of salt
1 tsp baking powder
100 g/3½ oz butter, cut into
    small pieces
150 g/5½ oz soft brown sugar
1 egg, beaten
4 tbsp milk
100 g/3½ oz hazelnuts, halved
demerara sugar, for sprinkling
    (optional)

method

1 Preheat the oven to 180°C/350°F/Gas Mark 4. Grease a 23-cm/9-inch square cake tin and line the base with baking paper.

2 Sift the flour, salt and baking powder into a large mixing bowl. Rub in the butter with your fingers until the mixture resembles fine breadcrumbs. Stir in the brown sugar. Add the egg, milk and nuts to the mixture and stir well until thoroughly combined.

3 Spoon the mixture into the prepared cake tin and level the surface. Sprinkle with demerara sugar, if using.

4 Bake in the preheated oven, for about 25 minutes, or until the mixture is firm to the touch when pressed with a finger.

5 Leave to cool for 10 minutes, then loosen the edges with a round-bladed knife and turn out onto a wire rack. Cut into squares.

honeyed apple slices

ingredients

makes 12

oil or melted butter,
   for greasing
175 g/6 oz plain white flour
2 tsp baking powder
½ tsp ground allspice
175 g/6 oz unsalted butter,
   softened
175 g/6 oz caster sugar
3 eggs, beaten
1 tsp vanilla extract
2 tbsp apple juice
4 red-skinned apples
3 tbsp clear honey, warmed

method

1 Preheat the oven to 180°C/350°F/Gas Mark 4. Grease and line a 30- x 23-cm/12- x 9-inch rectangular cake tin.

2 Sift the flour, baking powder and allspice into a large bowl and add the butter, sugar, eggs and vanilla extract. Beat well until the mixture is smooth, then stir in the apple juice.

3 Spoon the mixture into the prepared tin and smooth the surface with a palette knife. Core and slice the apples and arrange them, overlapping, on top of the cake mixture, without pressing into the mix. Brush lightly with half the honey.

4 Bake in the preheated oven for 30–35 minutes, or until risen, firm and golden brown. Leave to cool in the tin for about 15 minutes, until firm, then cut into slices and finish cooling on a wire rack.

5 Brush with the remaining honey before serving.

coconut bars

ingredients

makes 10

125 g/4½ oz unsalted butter,
    plus extra for greasing
225 g/8 oz golden caster sugar
2 eggs, beaten
finely grated rind of 1 orange
3 tbsp orange juice
150 ml/5 fl oz soured cream
140 g/5 oz self-raising flour
85 g/3 oz desiccated coconut
toasted shredded coconut,
    to decorate

frosting

1 egg white
200 g/7 oz icing sugar
85 g/3 oz desiccated coconut
about 1 tbsp orange juice

method

1 Preheat the oven to 180°C/350°F/Gas Mark 4. Grease a 23-cm/9-inch square cake tin and line the base with non-stick baking paper.

2 Cream together the butter and caster sugar until pale and fluffy, then gradually beat in the eggs. Stir in the orange rind, orange juice and soured cream. Fold in the flour and desiccated coconut evenly using a metal spoon.

3 Spoon the mixture into the prepared cake tin and level the surface. Bake in the preheated oven for 35–40 minutes, or until risen and firm to the touch.

4 Leave to cool for 10 minutes in the tin, then turn out and finish cooling on a wire rack.

5 For the frosting, lightly beat the egg white, just enough to break it up, and stir in the icing sugar and desiccated coconut, adding enough orange juice to mix to a thick paste. Spread over the top of the cake, sprinkle with toasted shredded coconut, then leave to set before slicing into bars.

coconut lamingtons

ingredients

makes 16

oil or melted butter,
    for greasing
175 g/6 oz plain white flour
1 tbsp baking powder
175 g/6 oz unsalted butter,
    softened
175 g/6 oz caster sugar
3 eggs, beaten
1 tsp vanilla extract
2 tbsp milk
2 tbsp desiccated coconut

icing & coating

500 g/1 lb 2 oz icing sugar
40 g/1½ oz cocoa powder
85 ml/3 fl oz boiling water
70 g/2½ oz unsalted butter,
    melted
250 g/9 oz desiccated coconut

method

1 Preheat the oven to 180°C/350°F/Gas Mark 4. Grease and line a 23-cm/9-inch square cake tin.

2 Sift the flour and baking powder into a large bowl and add the butter, caster sugar, eggs and vanilla extract. Beat well until the mixture is smooth, then stir in the milk and coconut.

3 Spoon the mixture into the prepared tin and smooth the surface with a palette knife. Bake in the preheated oven for 30–35 minutes, or until risen, firm and golden brown.

4 Leave to cool in the tin for 10 minutes, then turn out and finish cooling on a wire rack. When the cake is cold, cut into 16 squares with a sharp knife.

5 For the icing, sift the icing sugar and cocoa into a bowl. Add the water and butter and stir until smooth. Spread out the coconut on a large plate. Dip each piece of sponge cake into the icing, holding with two forks to coat evenly, then toss in coconut to cover. Place on a sheet of baking paper and leave to set.

variation

For a traditional filling, cut the lamingtons in half and fill with fresh whipped cream or jam – or both.

cinnamon squares

ingredients

makes 16

225 g/8 oz butter, softened,
plus extra for greasing
225 g/8 oz caster sugar
3 eggs, lightly beaten
225 g/8 oz self-raising flour
½ tsp bicarbonate of soda
1 tbsp ground cinnamon
150 ml/5 fl oz soured cream
55 g/2 oz sunflower seeds

method

1 Preheat the oven to 180°C/350°F/Gas Mark 4. Grease a 23-cm/9-inch square cake tin and line the base with baking paper.

2 In a large mixing bowl, cream together the butter and caster sugar until the mixture is light and fluffy. Gradually add the eggs to the mixture, beating thoroughly after each addition. Sift the flour, bicarbonate of soda and cinnamon together into the creamed mixture and fold in evenly using a metal spoon. Spoon in the soured cream and sunflower seeds and mix gently until well combined.

3 Spoon the mixture into the prepared tin and smooth the surface with the back of a spoon or a knife. Bake in the preheated oven for about 45 minutes, until the mixture is firm to the touch. Loosen the edges with a round-bladed knife, then turn out onto a wire rack to cool completely. Slice into squares before serving.

mango cakes

ingredients

makes 12

70 g/2½ oz dried mango,
    finely chopped
finely grated rind of 1 orange,
    plus 3 tbsp juice
25 g/1 oz creamed coconut
85 g/3 oz lightly salted butter,
    softened, plus extra for
    greasing
70 g/2½ oz caster sugar
1 egg
85 g/3 oz self-raising flour
icing sugar, for dusting

method

1 Preheat the oven to 180°C/350°F/Gas Mark 4. Place a
  12-section silicone mini loaf tray on a baking tray, or
  grease and base-line individual mini loaf tins. Put the
  mango and orange juice in a small bowl and leave to
  stand, covered, for 2–3 hours, or until the orange juice
  is mostly absorbed. Finely grate the coconut (if it's
  very firm and difficult to grate, warm it briefly in the
  microwave first).

2 Put the coconut, butter, sugar, egg, flour and orange
  rind in a mixing bowl and beat together with an
  electric whisk until smooth and pale. Stir in the mango
  and any unabsorbed orange juice.

3 Using a teaspoon, spoon the mixture into the tray
  sections and level with the back of the spoon. Bake
  in the preheated oven for 20 minutes (25 minutes if
  using tins), or until risen and just firm to the touch.
  Leave in the tray for 5 minutes, then transfer to a wire
  rack to cool.

4 Serve lightly dusted with icing sugar.

chocolate

white chocolate coffee gâteau

ingredients

serves 8–10

40 g/1½ oz unsalted butter,
  plus extra for greasing
85 g/3 oz white chocolate,
  broken into pieces
125 g/4½ oz caster sugar
4 large eggs, beaten
2 tbsp very strong black coffee
1 tsp vanilla extract
125 g/4½ oz plain flour
white chocolate curls, to decorate

frosting

175 g/6 oz white chocolate,
  broken into pieces
85 g/3 oz unsalted butter
125 g/4½ oz crème fraîche
125 g/4½ oz icing sugar, sifted
1 tbsp coffee liqueur or very
  strong black coffee

method

1 Preheat the oven to 180°C/350°F/Gas Mark 4. Grease two 20-cm/8-inch sandwich tins and line the bases with baking paper.

2 Place the butter and chocolate in a bowl set over a saucepan of hot water and leave on a very low heat until just melted. Stir, then remove from the heat.

3 Place the caster sugar, eggs, coffee and vanilla extract in a large bowl set over a saucepan of hot water and whisk hard with an electric whisk until the mixture is pale and thick. Remove from the heat, sift in the flour and fold in lightly. Fold in the butter and chocolate mixture, then divide the mixture between the prepared tins. Bake in the preheated oven for 25–30 minutes, until golden brown and springy to the touch. Leave to cool slightly, then turn out onto a wire rack to cool.

4 For the frosting, place the chocolate and butter in a bowl set over a saucepan of hot water and heat gently until melted. Remove from the heat, stir in the crème fraîche, icing sugar and coffee liqueur. Chill, stirring occasionally, until the mixture becomes thick and glossy. Sandwich the cakes together with some of the frosting and spread the remainder over the top and sides, swirling with a palette knife. Arrange the chocolate curls over the top of the cake and leave to set.

rich chocolate rum torte

ingredients

serves 8

oil or melted butter,
    for greasing
70 g/2½ oz plain chocolate,
    broken into pieces
2 tbsp milk
175 g/6 oz plain flour
1 tbsp baking powder
175 g/6 oz unsalted
    butter, softened
175 g/6 oz dark muscovado
    sugar
3 eggs, beaten
1 tsp vanilla extract
chocolate curls or grated
    chocolate, to decorate

frosting

225 g/8 oz plain chocolate,
    broken into pieces
225 ml/8 fl oz double cream
2 tbsp dark rum

method

1 Preheat the oven to 180°C/350°F/Gas Mark 4. Grease three 18-cm/7-inch sandwich tins and line with baking paper.

2 Place the chocolate and milk in a small saucepan and heat gently, without boiling, until melted. Stir and remove from the heat.

3 Sift the flour and baking powder into a large bowl and add the butter, sugar, eggs and vanilla extract. Beat well until smooth, then stir in the chocolate mixture.

4 Divide the mixture between the prepared tins and smooth level. Bake in the preheated oven for 20–25 minutes, until risen and firm to the touch. Leave to cool in the tins for 5 minutes, then turn out onto wire racks to finish cooling.

5 For the frosting, melt the chocolate with the cream and rum in a small saucepan over a low heat. Remove from the heat and leave to cool, stirring occasionally, until it reaches a spreadable consistency. Sandwich the cakes together with about a third of the frosting, then spread the remainder over the top and sides of the cake, swirling with a palette knife. Sprinkle with chocolate curls and leave to set.

chocolate & almond layer cake

ingredients

serves 10–12

oil or melted butter,
    for greasing
7 eggs
200 g/7 oz caster sugar
150 g/5½ oz plain flour
50 g/1¾ oz cocoa powder
50 g/1¾ oz butter, melted
75 g/2¾ oz toasted flaked
    almonds, crushed lightly and
    chocolate curls, to decorate

filling & topping

200 g/7 oz plain chocolate,
    broken into pieces
125 g/4½ oz butter
50 g/1¾ oz icing sugar

method

1 Preheat the oven to 180°C/350°F/Gas Mark 4. Grease a deep 23-cm/9-inch square cake tin and line the base with baking paper.

2 Whisk the eggs and caster sugar in a mixing bowl with an electric whisk for about 10 minutes, or until the mixture is very light and foamy and the whisk leaves a trail that lasts a few seconds when lifted.

3 Sift the flour and cocoa together and fold half into the mixture. Drizzle over the melted butter and fold in the rest of the flour and cocoa. Pour into the prepared tin and bake in the preheated oven for 30–35 minutes, or until springy to the touch. Leave the cake to cool in the tin for 5 minutes, then turn out onto a wire rack to finish cooling.

4 For the filling and topping, melt the chocolate and butter together, then remove from the heat. Stir in the icing sugar, leave to cool, then beat until thick enough to spread.

5 Halve the cake lengthways and cut each half into 3 layers. Sandwich the layers together with three quarters of the chocolate mixture. Spread the remainder over the cake and mark a wavy pattern on the top. To decorate, press the almonds onto the sides and sprinkle with the chocolate curls.

chocolate & cherry gâteau

ingredients

serves 8

oil or melted butter,
    for greasing
150 g/5½ oz plain flour
2 tbsp cocoa powder
1 tbsp baking powder
175 g/6 oz unsalted butter,
    softened
175 g/6 oz golden caster sugar
3 eggs, beaten
1 tsp vanilla extract
2 tbsp milk
3 tbsp kirsch or brandy
    (optional)
grated chocolate and fresh
    whole cherries, to decorate

filling & topping

450 ml/16 fl oz double
    or whipping cream
2 tbsp icing sugar
225 g/8 oz fresh dark red
    cherries, stoned

method

1 Preheat the oven to 180°C/350°F/Gas Mark 4. Grease
    two 20-cm/8-inch sandwich tins and line the bases
    with baking paper.

2 Sift the flour, cocoa and baking powder into a large
    bowl and add the butter, caster sugar, eggs and vanilla
    extract. Beat well until the mixture is smooth, then stir
    in the milk.

3 Divide the mixture between the prepared tins and
    smooth level. Bake in the preheated oven for 25–30
    minutes, or until risen and firm to the touch. Leave
    to cool in the tins for 2–3 minutes, then turn out and
    finish cooling on wire racks.

4 When the cakes are cold, sprinkle with the kirsch, if
    using. For the filling and topping, whip the cream with
    the icing sugar until thick, then spread about a third
    over the top of one of the cakes. Spread the cherries
    among the cream and place the second cake on top.

5 Spread the remaining cream over the top and sides of
    the cake and decorate with grated chocolate and fresh
    whole cherries.

black forest roulade

ingredients

serves 8–10

sunflower oil, for greasing
175 g/6 oz plain chocolate
2–3 tbsp kirsch or brandy
5 eggs
225 g/8 oz caster sugar
icing sugar, for dusting

filling

350 ml/12 fl oz double cream
1–2 tbsp kirsch or brandy
350 g/12 oz fresh black cherries,
    stoned, or 400 g/14 oz canned
    morello cherries, drained and
    stoned

method

1 Preheat the oven to 190°C/375°F/Gas Mark 5. Grease and line a 35- x 25-cm/14- x 10-inch Swiss roll tin.

2 Break the chocolate into small pieces and place in a heatproof bowl set over a saucepan of gently simmering water. Add the kirsch and heat slowly, stirring until the mixture is smooth. Remove from the pan and set aside.

3 Place the eggs and caster sugar in a large heatproof bowl and set over the pan of gently simmering water. Whisk the eggs and sugar until very thick and creamy. Remove the bowl from the heat and whisk in the cooled chocolate mixture.

4 Spoon into the prepared tin, then tap the tin lightly on the work surface to smooth the top. Bake in the preheated oven for 20 minutes, or until firm to the touch. Remove from the oven and turn onto a sheet of baking paper, dusted with the icing sugar. Lift off the tin and lining paper, then roll up, encasing the baking paper in the roulade. Leave until cold.

5 For the filling, whip the cream until soft peaks form, then stir in the kirsch. Unroll the roulade and spread over the cream to within 5 mm/¼ inch of the edges. Scatter the cherries over the cream. Carefully roll up the roulade again and place on a serving platter.

double chocolate mint sponge

ingredients

serves 8

oil or melted butter,
    for greasing
150 g/5½ oz plain flour
2 tbsp cocoa powder
1 tbsp baking powder
175 g/6 oz unsalted butter,
    softened
175 g/6 oz caster sugar
3 eggs, beaten
1 tbsp milk
40 g/1½ oz chocolate mint
    sticks, chopped
140 g/5 oz chocolate spread,
    plus extra to drizzle
chocolate mint sticks,
    to decorate

method

1 Preheat the oven to 180°C/350°F/Gas Mark 4. Grease two 20-cm/8-inch sandwich tins and line with baking paper.

2 Sift the flour, cocoa and baking powder into a bowl and beat in the butter, sugar and eggs, mixing until smooth. Stir in the milk and chocolate mint pieces.

3 Spread the mixture into the prepared tins. Bake in the preheated oven for 25–30 minutes, until risen and firm. Cool in the tin for 2 minutes, then turn out onto a wire rack to finish cooling.

4 Sandwich the cakes together with chocolate spread and decorate with chocolate mint sticks. Drizzle chocolate spread over the top.

hot chocolate cheesecake

ingredients

serves 8–10

oil or melted butter,
    for greasing
150 g/5½ oz plain flour,
    plus extra for dusting
2 tbsp cocoa powder
55 g/2 oz butter
2 tbsp golden caster sugar
25 g/1 oz ground almonds
1 egg yolk
icing sugar, for dusting
grated chocolate, to decorate

filling

2 eggs, separated
75 g/2¾ oz golden caster sugar
350 g/12 oz cream cheese
4 tbsp ground almonds
150 ml/5 fl oz double cream
25 g/1 oz cocoa powder, sifted
1 tsp vanilla extract

method

1 Grease a 20-cm/8-inch loose-based round cake tin.

2 Sift the flour and cocoa into a bowl and rub in the butter with your fingertips until the mixture resembles fine breadcrumbs. Stir in the sugar and ground almonds. Add the egg yolk and enough water to make a soft dough.

3 Roll out the pastry on a lightly floured work surface and use to line the prepared tin. Leave to chill for 30 minutes. Preheat the oven to 160°C/325°F/Gas Mark 3.

4 For the filling, put the egg yolks and sugar in a large bowl and whisk until thick and pale. Whisk in the cream cheese, ground almonds, cream, cocoa and vanilla extract until well combined.

5 Put the egg whites in a large bowl and whisk until stiff but not dry. Stir a little of the egg whites into the cheese mixture, then fold in the remainder. Pour into the pastry case.

6 Bake in the preheated oven for 1½ hours, until well risen and just firm to the touch. Leave to cool slightly, then carefully remove from the tin, dust with icing sugar and sprinkle with grated chocolate. Serve the cheesecake warm.

chocolate cake with syrup

ingredients

serves 12

oil or melted butter,
    for greasing
225 g/8 oz plain chocolate,
    broken into pieces
115 g/4 oz butter
1 tbsp strong black coffee
4 large eggs
2 egg yolks
115 g/4 oz caster sugar
40 g/1½ oz plain flour
2 tsp ground cinnamon
85 g/3 oz ground almonds
chocolate-covered coffee
    beans, to decorate

syrup
300 ml/10 fl oz strong
    black coffee
115 g/4 oz caster sugar
1 cinnamon stick

method

1 Preheat the oven to 190°C/375°F/Gas Mark 5. Grease a 20-cm/8-inch round deep cake tin and line with baking paper.

2 Place the chocolate, butter and coffee in a heatproof bowl and set over a saucepan of gently simmering water until melted. Stir to blend, then remove from the heat and leave to cool slightly.

3 Place the whole eggs, egg yolks and sugar in a separate bowl and whisk together until thick and pale. Sift the flour and cinnamon over the egg mixture. Add the almonds and the chocolate mixture and fold in carefully. Spoon the mixture into the prepared tin. Bake in the preheated oven for 35 minutes, or until the tip of a knife inserted into the centre comes out clean. Leave to cool slightly before turning out on to a serving plate.

4 For the syrup, place the coffee, sugar and cinnamon stick in a heavy-based saucepan and heat gently, stirring, until the sugar has dissolved. Increase the heat and boil for 5 minutes, or until reduced and thickened slightly. Keep warm. Pierce the surface of the cake with a cocktail stick, then drizzle over half the coffee syrup. Decorate with chocolate-covered coffee beans and serve, cut into wedges, with the remaining coffee syrup.

chocolate sandwich cake

ingredients

serves 8

oil or melted butter,
    for greasing
150 g/5½ oz plain flour
2 tbsp cocoa powder
1 tbsp baking powder
175 g/6 oz unsalted butter,
    softened
175 g/6 oz golden caster sugar
3 eggs, beaten
1 tsp vanilla extract
2 tbsp milk
140 g/5 oz chocolate spread
icing sugar, for dusting

method

1 Preheat the oven to 180°C/350°F/Gas Mark 4. Grease
two 20-cm/8-inch sandwich tins and line the bases
with baking paper.

2 Sift the flour, cocoa and baking powder into a large
bowl and add the butter, caster sugar, eggs and vanilla
extract. Beat well until the mixture is smooth, then stir
in the milk.

3 Divide the mixture between the prepared tins and
smooth level. Bake in the preheated oven for 25–30
minutes, or until well risen and firm to the touch. Leave
to cool in the tins for 2–3 minutes, then turn out onto
a wire rack to finish cooling.

4 When the cakes have cooled completely, sandwich
together with the chocolate spread, then dust with
icing sugar and serve.

variation

For a more luxurious cake, replace the chocolate
spread filling and icing sugar dusting with
300 ml/10 fl oz whipped cream. Before serving,
arrange sliced strawberries on the top.

dotty chocolate chip cake

ingredients

serves 10

175 g/6 oz soft margarine
or spreadable butter,
plus extra for greasing
175 g/6 oz caster sugar
3 eggs, beaten
175 g/6 oz plain flour
1 tsp baking powder
2 tbsp cocoa powder
55 g/2 oz white chocolate chips
40 g/1½ oz small coloured sweets,
to decorate

icing

175 g/6 oz milk chocolate or
plain chocolate, broken into
pieces
100 g/3½ oz unsalted butter
or margarine
1 tbsp golden syrup

method

1 Preheat the oven to 160°C/325°F/Gas Mark 3. Grease a 20-cm/8-inch round cake tin and line the base with baking paper.

2 Place the margarine, sugar, eggs, flour, baking powder and cocoa powder in a bowl and beat until just smooth. Stir in the chocolate chips, mixing evenly.

3 Spoon the mixture into the prepared tin and spread the top level. Bake in the preheated oven for 40–45 minutes, until risen and firm to the touch. Leave to cool in the tin for 5 minutes, then turn out and finish cooling completely on a wire rack.

4 For the icing, place the chocolate, butter and golden syrup in a saucepan over a low heat and stir until just melted and smooth.

5 Remove from the heat and leave to cool until it begins to thicken enough to leave a trail when the spoon is lifted. Pour the icing over the top of the cake, allowing it to drizzle down the sides. Arrange the sweets over the top of the cake.

marbled chocolate & vanilla ring

ingredients

serves 12

oil or melted butter,
   for greasing
175 g/6 oz plain white flour
1 tbsp baking powder
175 g/6 oz unsalted butter,
   softened
175 g/6 oz caster sugar
3 eggs, beaten
2 tbsp cocoa powder
2 tbsp milk
1 tsp vanilla extract
icing sugar, for dusting

method

1 Preheat the oven to 160°C/325°F/Gas Mark 3. Grease a 1.5-litre/2¾-pint ring cake tin, preferably non-stick.

2 Sift the flour and baking powder into a large bowl and add the butter, caster sugar and eggs. Beat well until the mixture is smooth. Transfer half the mixture to a separate bowl.

3 Mix the cocoa powder with the milk and stir into one bowl of mixture. Add the vanilla extract to the other bowl and mix evenly. Spoon alternate tablespoons of the two mixtures into the prepared tin and swirl lightly with a palette knife for a marbled effect.

4 Bake in the preheated oven for 40–50 minutes, or until risen, firm and golden brown. Leave to cool in the tin for 10 minutes, then turn out and finish cooling on a wire rack. Dust with icing sugar before serving.

chocolate ganache cake

ingredients

serves 10

175 g/6 oz butter, plus extra
  for greasing
175 g/6 oz caster sugar
4 eggs, lightly beaten
200 g/7 oz self-raising flour
1 tbsp cocoa powder
50 g/1¾ oz plain chocolate,
  melted

ganache

450 ml/16 fl oz double cream
375 g/13 oz plain chocolate,
  broken into pieces
200 g/7 oz chocolate-flavoured
  cake covering, to finish

method

1 Lightly grease and base-line a 20-cm/8-inch springform cake tin. Beat the butter and sugar until light and fluffy. Gradually add the eggs, beating well. Sift the flour and cocoa together. Fold into the cake mixture. Fold in the melted chocolate. Pour the mixture into the prepared tin and smooth the top.

2 Bake in a preheated oven, 180°C/350°F/Gas Mark 4, for 40 minutes, or until springy to the touch. Cool for 5 minutes in the tin, then turn out onto a wire rack to cool completely. Cut the cold cake into two layers.

3 To make the ganache, place the cream in a saucepan and bring to the boil, stirring. Add the chocolate and stir until melted and combined. Pour into a bowl and whisk for about 5 minutes or until fluffy and cool. Set aside one third of the ganache and use the rest to sandwich the cake together and spread smoothly and evenly over the top and sides of the cake.

4 Melt the cake covering and spread it over a large sheet of baking parchment. Cool until just set. Cut into strips a little wider than the height of the cake. Place them around the edge of the cake, overlapping slightly.

5 Using a piping bag with a fine nozzle, pipe the reserved ganache in tear drops or shells to cover the top of the cake. Chill for 1 hour in the refrigerator before serving.

warm white chocolate macadamia ring

ingredients

serves 8

oil or melted butter,
    for greasing
70 g/2½ oz white chocolate,
    broken into pieces
2 tbsp milk
1 tsp vanilla extract
175 g/6 oz plain white flour
1 tbsp baking powder
175 g/6 oz unsalted butter,
    softened
175 g/6 oz caster sugar
3 eggs, beaten
55 g/2 oz macadamia nuts,
    finely chopped, plus extra
    to decorate

sauce

100 g/3½ oz white chocolate,
    broken into pieces
125 ml/4 fl oz single cream
½ tsp vanilla extract

method

1 Preheat the oven to 180°C/350°F/Gas Mark 4. Grease a 1.5-litre/2¾-pint ring cake tin, preferably non-stick.

2 Place the chocolate, milk and vanilla extract in a small pan and heat gently, stirring occasionally, until just melted and smooth. Remove from the heat.

3 Sift the flour and baking powder into a large bowl and add the butter, sugar and eggs. Beat well until the mixture is smooth, then beat in the melted chocolate mixture. Stir in the macadamia nuts, mixing evenly.

4 Spoon the mixture into the prepared tin and smooth the surface with a palette knife. Bake in the preheated oven for 35–40 minutes, or until risen, firm and golden brown.

5 For the sauce, place the chocolate, cream and vanilla extract in a saucepan and heat gently until melted and smooth.

6 Leave the cake to cool in the tin for 2–3 minutes, then turn out carefully onto a warmed serving plate. Drizzle the sauce over the cake and sprinkle with macadamia nuts, then serve in thick slices.

gooey orange chocolate chip cake

ingredients

serves 6

oil or melted butter,
    for greasing
2 oranges
175 g/6 oz plain white flour
2 tsp baking powder
175 g/6 oz unsalted butter,
    softened
175 g/6 oz golden caster sugar
3 eggs, beaten
1 tsp vanilla extract
100 g/3½ oz plain chocolate chips

sauce

85 g/3 oz plain chocolate,
    broken into pieces
40 g/1½ oz unsalted butter
3 tbsp orange juice

method

1 Preheat the oven to 180°C/350°F/Gas Mark 4. Grease and line a 23-cm/9-inch square cake tin.

2 Finely grate the rind from one of the oranges and reserve. Use a sharp knife to cut off all the peel and white pith from both oranges and carefully remove the segments, reserving any spare juices to add to the sauce. Chop half the segments into small pieces.

3 Sift the flour and baking powder into a large bowl and add the butter, sugar, eggs and vanilla extract. Beat well until the mixture is smooth, then stir in the orange rind and chopped orange.

4 Spoon the mixture into the prepared tin and smooth the surface with a palette knife. Sprinkle the chocolate chips over the top, spreading to the edges with a palette knife. Bake in the preheated oven for 35–40 minutes, or until risen, firm and golden brown.

5 For the sauce, place the chocolate, butter and orange juice in a saucepan and heat gently, stirring, until melted and smooth. Serve the cake warm, topped with the reserved orange segments and with the sauce spooned over the top.

chocolate mint cake pops

ingredients

makes 26–28

300 g/10½ oz plain chocolate,
  roughly chopped
25 g/1 oz unsalted butter,
  softened
50 g/1¾ oz hard-boiled mint
  sweets
450 g/1 lb milk chocolate
50 g/1¾ oz mini marshmallows,
  roughly chopped
26–28 lolly sticks
chocolate sprinkles, to decorate

method

1 Line a baking tray with baking paper. Put the plain chocolate in a heatproof bowl, set the bowl over a saucepan of gently simmering water and heat until melted. Stir in the butter. Leave until the mixture is cool but not beginning to set.

2 Put the mint sweets in a polythene bag and tap firmly with a rolling pin until they are broken into tiny pieces. Finely chop 150 g/5½ oz of the milk chocolate, then stir it into the melted plain chocolate with the mints and marshmallows until thoroughly mixed.

3 As soon as the mixture is firm enough to hold its shape, roll 20 g/¾ oz of it into a ball. Shape the remaining cake pops in the same way. Place them on the baking tray and chill for 30–60 minutes, until firm but not brittle. Push a lolly stick into each cake pop, then chill for 10 minutes.

4 Roughly chop the remaining milk chocolate and melt as above, then remove from the heat. Dip a cake pop into the chocolate, turning it until coated. Lift it from the bowl, letting the excess drip back into the bowl, and place it in a cup or tumbler. Sprinkle with chocolate sprinkles. Repeat with the remaining cake pops. Chill or leave in a cool place until the chocolate has set.

mont blanc macaroons

ingredients

makes 6

75 g/2¾ oz ground almonds
100 g/3½ oz icing sugar,
    plus extra for dusting
2 tbsp cocoa powder
2 large egg whites
50 g/1¾ oz caster sugar

filling

200 ml/7 fl oz double cream
4 tbsp sweetened
    chestnut purée
2 tbsp plain chocolate shavings

method

1 Place the ground almonds, icing sugar and cocoa powder in a food processor and process for 15 seconds. Sift the mixture into a bowl. Line two baking sheets with baking paper.

2 Place the egg whites in a large bowl and whisk until holding soft peaks. Whisk in the caster sugar to make a firm, glossy meringue. Using a spatula, fold the almond mixture into the meringue one third at a time. When all the dry ingredients are thoroughly incorporated, continue to cut and fold the mixture until it forms a shiny batter with a thick, ribbon-like consistency.

3 Pour the mixture into a piping bag fitted with a 1-cm/½-inch plain nozzle. Pipe 12 large rounds onto the prepared baking sheets. Leave at room temperature for 30 minutes. Preheat the oven to 160°C/325°F/Gas Mark 3.

4 Bake in the preheated oven for 15–20 minutes. Cool for 10 minutes and then carefully peel the macaroons off the baking paper. Leave to cool completely.

5 For the filling, whip the cream until holding soft peaks and fold into the chestnut purée. Pipe the chestnut mixture onto half the macaroons. Top with chocolate shavings and the remaining macaroon shells. Serve dusted with icing sugar.

chocolate whoopie pies

ingredients

makes 10

175 g/6 oz plain flour

1½ tsp bicarbonate of soda

40 g/1½ oz cocoa powder

large pinch of salt

85 g/3 oz butter, softened

85 g/3 oz white vegetable fat

150 g/5½ oz soft dark brown
sugar

1 large egg, beaten

1 tsp vanilla extract

150 ml/5 fl oz milk

marshmallow filling

225 g/8 oz white marshmallows

4 tbsp milk

115 g/4 oz white vegetable fat

55 g/2 oz icing sugar, sifted

method

1 Preheat the oven to 180°C/350°F/Gas Mark 4. Line 2–3 large baking sheets with baking paper. Sift together the plain flour, bicarbonate of soda, cocoa powder and salt.

2 Place the butter, white vegetable fat and sugar in a large bowl and beat with an electric whisk until pale and fluffy. Beat in the egg and vanilla extract followed by half the flour mixture and then the milk. Stir in the rest of the flour mixture and mix together until thoroughly incorporated.

3 Pipe or spoon 20 mounds of the mixture onto the prepared baking sheets, spaced well apart to allow for spreading. Bake in the preheated oven, one sheet at a time, for 12–14 minutes until risen and just firm to the touch. Cool for 5 minutes, then using a palette knife transfer to a wire rack and leave to cool completely.

4 For the filling, place the marshmallows and milk in a heatproof bowl set over a pan of simmering water. Leave until the marshmallows have melted, stirring occasionally. Remove from the heat and leave to cool.

5 Place the white vegetable fat and icing sugar in a bowl and beat together until smooth and creamy. Add the creamed mixture to the marshmallow and beat for 1–2 minutes until fluffy. Spread the filling over the flat side of half the cakes. Top with the rest of the cakes.

chocolate & lime whoopie pies

ingredients

makes 10

250 g/9 oz plain flour
1 tsp bicarbonate of soda
25 g/1 oz cocoa powder
large pinch of salt
115 g/4 oz butter, softened
150 g/5½ oz caster sugar
1 large egg, beaten
1 tsp vanilla extract
4 tbsp soured cream
3 tbsp milk

filling

175 g/6 oz full-fat soft cheese
85 g/3 oz unsalted butter, softened
finely grated rind and juice
    of 1 lime
115 g/4 oz icing sugar, sifted

glaze

85 g/3 oz plain chocolate,
    broken into pieces
55 g/ 2 oz unsalted butter

method

1 Preheat the oven to 180°C/350°F/Gas Mark 4. Line 2–3 large baking sheets with baking paper. Sift together the plain flour, bicarbonate of soda, cocoa and salt.

2 Place the butter and sugar in a large bowl and beat with an electric whisk until pale and fluffy. Beat in the caster sugar, egg and vanilla extract followed by half the flour mixture then the soured cream and milk. Stir in the rest of the flour mixture and mix until thoroughly incorporated.

3 Pipe or spoon 20 mounds of the mixture onto the prepared baking sheets, spaced well apart to allow for spreading. Bake, one sheet at a time, in the preheated oven for 10–12 minutes until risen and just firm to the touch. Cool for 5 minutes, then using a palette knife transfer to a wire rack and leave to cool completely.

4 For the filling, place the soft cheese and butter in a bowl and beat with an electric whisk for 2–3 minutes until pale and creamy. Gradually beat in the lime juice, rind and icing sugar and continue beating for 2–3 minutes until the buttercream is very light and fluffy.

5 Melt the chocolate with the butter. To assemble, spread or pipe the buttercream on the flat side of half of the cakes. Sandwich the cakes together and decorate one half of each pie with the chocolate glaze.

chocolate chip whoopie pies

ingredients

makes 10

250 g/9 oz plain flour
1 tsp bicarbonate of soda
large pinch of salt
115 g/4 oz butter, softened
150 g/5½ oz soft light
    brown sugar
1 large egg, beaten
1 tsp vanilla extract
150 ml/5 fl oz soured cream
85 g/3 oz milk chocolate chips

filling

150 g/5½ oz plain chocolate,
    broken into pieces
115 g/4 oz unsalted butter,
    softened
150 ml/5 fl oz double cream

method

1 Preheat the oven to 180°C/350°F/Gas Mark 4. Line 2–3 large baking sheets with baking paper. Sift together the plain flour, bicarbonate of soda and salt.

2 Place the butter and sugar in a large bowl and beat with an electric whisk until pale and fluffy. Whisk in the egg and vanilla extract, followed by half the flour mixture and then the soured cream. Stir in the rest of the flour mixture and mix until thoroughly incorporated. Stir in half the chocolate chips.

3 Pipe or spoon 20 mounds of the mixture onto the prepared baking sheets, spaced well apart to allow for spreading. Sprinkle over the rest of the chocolate chips. Bake in the preheated oven, one sheet at a time, for 10–12 minutes until risen and just firm to the touch. Cool for 5 minutes, then using a palette knife transfer to a wire rack and leave to cool completely.

4 For the filling, place the chocolate and butter in a heatproof bowl set over a pan of simmering water and leave until melted, stirring occasionally. Remove from the heat and leave to cool for 20 minutes. Stir the cream into the cooled chocolate then chill in the refrigerator for 10–15 minutes until firm enough to spread.

5 To assemble, spread the chocolate filling on the flat side of half of the cakes. Top with the rest of the cakes.

fruit

berry crunch cake

ingredients

serves 8

oil or melted butter,
  for greasing
175 g/6 oz plain white flour,
  plus 1 tbsp
2 tsp baking powder
175 g/6 oz unsalted butter,
  softened
175 g/6 oz caster sugar
3 eggs, beaten
1 tsp vanilla extract
225 g/8 oz fresh mixed berries,
  such as raspberries,
  blueberries and blackberries
70 g/2½ oz ginger nut biscuits,
  crushed

method

1 Preheat the oven to 180°C/350°F/Gas Mark 4. Grease a 23-cm/9-inch round springform cake tin and line the base with baking paper.

2 Sift 175 g/6 oz flour and baking powder into a large bowl and add the butter, sugar, eggs and vanilla extract. Beat well until the mixture is smooth.

3 Spoon about half the mixture into the prepared tin and smooth the surface with a palette knife. Spread the berries evenly over the mixture. Stir the extra tablespoon of flour into the remaining mix. Spread out the crushed biscuits on a large plate. Using two spoons, toss small spoonfuls of the mix in the crushed biscuits, then arrange over the cake. Sprinkle over any remaining biscuit crumbs.

4 Bake in the preheated oven for 45–55 minutes, or until risen, firm and golden brown. Leave to cool in the tin for 2–3 minutes, then remove the sides and finish cooling on a wire rack. This cake is best eaten on the day of making.

frosted raspberry almond ring

ingredients

serves 8–10

oil or melted butter,
 for greasing
175 g/6 oz plain white flour
1 tbsp baking powder
175 g/6 oz unsalted butter,
 softened
175 g/6 oz caster sugar
3 eggs, beaten
1 tsp almond extract
70 g/2½ oz ground almonds
140 g/5 oz fresh raspberries,
 plus extra to decorate
toasted flaked almonds,
 to decorate

frosting

1 large egg white
140 g/5 oz icing sugar
1 tbsp golden syrup
¼ tsp cream of tartar

method

1 Preheat the oven to 160°C/325°F/Gas Mark 3. Grease a 1.5-litre/2¾-pint ring cake tin, preferably non-stick.

2 Sift the flour and baking powder into a large bowl and add the butter, caster sugar, eggs and almond extract. Beat well until the mixture is smooth, then stir in the ground almonds. Mash half the raspberries with a fork and stir into the mixture.

3 Spoon the mixture into the prepared tin and smooth the surface with a palette knife. Bake in the preheated oven for 40–45 minutes, or until the cake is risen, firm and golden brown.

4 Leave to cool in the tin for 10 minutes, then turn out carefully onto a wire rack to finish cooling.

5 For the frosting, place the egg white, icing sugar, golden syrup and cream of tartar in a bowl over a saucepan of hot water and whisk vigorously with an electric mixer until thick enough to hold its shape.

6 Swirl the frosting over the top of the cake. Decorate with the remaining raspberries and the flaked almonds.

raspberry vacherin

ingredients

serves 10

3 egg whites
175 g/6 oz caster sugar
1 tsp cornflour
25 g/1 oz plain chocolate, grated

filling & topping
175 g/6 oz plain chocolate,
    broken into pieces
450 ml/16 fl oz double cream,
    whipped
280 g/10 oz fresh raspberries
a little melted chocolate,
    to decorate

method

1 Preheat the oven to 140°C/275°F/Gas Mark 1. Draw three rectangles, measuring 10 x 25 cm/4 x 10 inches, on baking paper and place on two baking trays.

2 Whisk the egg whites in a mixing bowl until soft peaks form, then gradually whisk in half the sugar and continue whisking until the mixture is very stiff and glossy. Fold in the remaining sugar, the cornflour and the grated chocolate. Spoon the meringue mixture into a piping bag fitted with a 1-cm/½-inch plain nozzle and pipe lines across the rectangles.

3 Bake in the preheated oven for 1½ hours. Turn off the oven and leave the meringues to cool inside the oven, then peel away the baking paper.

4 Place the chocolate in a heatproof bowl set over a saucepan of gently simmering water until melted. Spread the chocolate over two of the meringue layers. Leave to harden. Place one chocolate-coated meringue on a plate and top with about one third of the cream and raspberries. Gently place the second chocolate-coated meringue on top and spread with half of the remaining cream and raspberries. Place the last meringue on the top and decorate with the remaining cream and raspberries. Drizzle the melted chocolate over the top of the vacherin and serve.

strawberry sponge slices

ingredients

serves 6–8

oil or melted butter,
    for greasing
150 g/5½ oz plain white flour
1½ tsp baking powder
175 g/6 oz unsalted butter,
    softened
175 g/6 oz caster sugar
3 eggs, beaten
1 tsp vanilla extract
2 tbsp milk
250 g/9 oz fresh strawberries,
    plus extra for decorating
250 g/9 oz mascarpone cheese
icing sugar, for dusting

method

1 Preheat the oven to 180°C/350°F/Gas Mark 4. Grease
    and line a 23- x 33-cm/9- x 13-inch Swiss roll tin with
    the paper 1 cm/½ inch above the rim.

2 Sift the flour and baking powder into a large bowl
    and add the butter, sugar, eggs and vanilla extract.
    Beat well until the mixture is smooth, then beat in
    the milk.

3 Spoon the mixture into the prepared tin and smooth
    into the corners with a palette knife. Bake in the
    preheated oven for 15–20 minutes, or until risen,
    firm and golden brown. Leave to cool in the tin.

4 When the cake is cold, cut crossways into three
    rectangles. Hull and chop the strawberries, reserving
    a few whole for decoration. Stir the chopped
    strawberries into the mascarpone and use to sandwich
    together the cakes.

5 To serve, dust the cake with icing sugar. Hull and slice
    the reserved strawberries and arrange on top.

strawberry mousse cake

ingredients

serves 8–10

oil or melted butter,
    for greasing
175 g/6 oz plain flour
1 tbsp baking powder
175 g/6 oz unsalted butter,
    softened
175 g/6 oz golden caster sugar
3 eggs, beaten
1 tsp vanilla extract
2 tbsp milk

filling & topping

4 tsp powdered gelatine
3 tbsp orange juice
400 g/14 oz fresh strawberries,
    plus extra for decorating
3 tbsp golden caster sugar
400 ml/14 fl oz double cream
100 g/3½ oz redcurrant
    jelly, warmed

method

1 Preheat the oven to 160°C/325°F/Gas Mark 3. Grease a
    23-cm/9-inch round springform cake tin and line with
    baking paper.

2 Sift the flour and baking powder into a large bowl and
    add the butter, sugar, eggs and vanilla extract. Beat
    well until the mixture is smooth, then stir in the milk.
    Spoon the mixture into the prepared tin and smooth
    level. Bake in the preheated oven for 45–55 minutes,
    or until risen, firm and golden brown.

3 Leave to cool in the tin for 5 minutes, then turn out
    onto a wire rack to finish cooling. Cut the sponge in
    half horizontally and place one half back in the cake tin.

4 For the filling, dissolve the gelatine in the orange
    juice in a small bowl placed in a saucepan of hot water.
    In a blender or processor, purée the strawberries with
    the sugar. Whip the cream until thick enough to hold
    its shape. Quickly stir the gelatine mixture into the
    strawberry mixture, then fold in the cream.

5 Pour the mixture into the tin and place the second half
    of the cake on top. Chill in the refrigerator until set.
    Turn out the cake and spread the top with the warmed
    redcurrant jelly. Decorate the mousse cake with the
    remaining halved strawberries.

blueberry orange streusel cake

ingredients

serves 8–10

oil or melted butter,
    for greasing
175 g/6 oz plain white flour
2 tsp baking powder
175 g/6 oz unsalted butter,
    softened
175 g/6 oz caster sugar
3 eggs, beaten
1 tsp vanilla extract
finely grated rind of ½ orange
55 g/2 oz ground almonds
125 g/4½ oz fresh blueberries

topping

55 g/2 oz plain white flour
25 g/1 oz unsalted butter, softened
25 g/1 oz caster sugar
finely grated rind of ½ orange

method

1 Preheat the oven to 160°C/325°F/Gas Mark 3. Grease a 23-cm/9-inch round springform cake tin and line the base with baking paper.

2 For the topping, place all the ingredients in a bowl and mix with a fork to make a crumbly mixture.

3 Sift the flour and baking powder into a large bowl and add the butter, sugar, eggs and vanilla extract. Beat well until the mixture is smooth, then add the orange rind, ground almonds and half the blueberries.

4 Spoon the mixture into the prepared tin, smooth the surface with a palette knife and scatter over the remaining blueberries. Spread the crumble topping evenly over the top, covering completely.

5 Bake in the preheated oven for 1–1¼ hours, or until risen, firm and golden brown. Leave to cool in the tin for 10 minutes, then remove the sides of the tin and finish cooling on a wire rack.

pear & hazelnut streusel cake

ingredients

serves 8

oil or melted butter,
   for greasing
175 g/6 oz plain white flour
2 tsp baking powder
175 g/6 oz unsalted butter,
   softened
175 g/6 oz golden caster
   sugar
3 eggs, beaten
1 tsp vanilla extract
55 g/2 oz ground hazelnuts
2 firm ripe pears, peeled,
   cored and finely chopped

topping

50 g/1¾ oz toasted hazelnuts,
   finely chopped
40 g/1½ oz dark muscovado
   sugar
3 tbsp plain white flour
½ tsp ground cinnamon
25 g/1 oz unsalted butter,
   melted

method

1 Preheat the oven to 180°C/350°F/Gas Mark 4. Grease and line a 23-cm/9-inch round springform cake tin.

2 For the streusel topping, mix the chopped hazelnuts, muscovado sugar, flour, cinnamon and melted butter in a small bowl with a fork to make a crumbly mixture.

3 Sift the flour and baking powder into a large bowl and add the butter, caster sugar, eggs and vanilla extract. Beat well until the mixture is smooth, then stir in the ground hazelnuts and half the chopped pears.

4 Spoon the mixture into the prepared tin and smooth the surface with a palette knife. Scatter over the remaining chopped pears and spread level. Sprinkle the streusel topping evenly over the cake.

5 Bake in the preheated oven for about 1 hour, or until risen, firm and golden brown. Leave to cool in the tin for 2–3 minutes, then remove the sides of the tin and finish cooling on a wire rack.

peachy oat crumble cake

ingredients

serves 8–10

oil or melted butter,
    for greasing

175 g/6 oz plain white flour

1 tbsp baking powder

1 tsp ground star anise

175 g/6 oz unsalted butter,
    softened

175 g/6 oz golden caster sugar

3 eggs, beaten

1 tsp vanilla extract

4 ripe peaches, stoned and
    roughly chopped

topping

125 g/4½ oz porridge oats

55 g/2 oz golden caster sugar

55 g/2 oz unsalted butter, melted

method

1 Preheat the oven to 180°C/350°F/Gas Mark 4. Grease a 25-cm/10-inch round springform cake tin and line the base with baking paper.

2 Sift the flour, baking powder and star anise into a large bowl and add the butter, sugar, eggs and vanilla extract. Beat well until the mixture is smooth.

3 Spoon the mixture into the prepared tin and smooth the surface with a palette knife. Arrange the chopped peaches evenly over the top.

4 For the topping, mix together the oats and sugar in a small bowl, then stir in the melted butter to make a crumbly mix. Spread evenly over the peaches.

5 Bake in the preheated oven for about 1 hour, or until risen, firm and golden brown. Leave to cool in the tin for 2–3 minutes, then remove the sides and finish cooling on a wire rack. This cake is best eaten on the day of making.

peach & cinnamon pie

ingredients

serves 6

oil or melted butter,
    for greasing
175 g/6 oz plain white flour
2 tsp baking powder
1 tsp ground cinnamon
175 g/6 oz unsalted butter,
    softened
175 g/6 oz golden caster sugar
3 eggs, beaten
1 tsp vanilla extract
3 ripe peaches or nectarines,
    stoned and roughly chopped
70 g/2½ oz cornflakes,
    lightly crushed
lightly whipped cream, to serve

method

1 Preheat the oven to 160°C/325°F/Gas Mark 3. Grease a 23-cm/9-inch round springform cake tin and line the base with baking paper.

2 Sift the flour, baking powder and cinnamon into a large bowl and add the butter, sugar, eggs and vanilla extract. Beat well until the mixture is smooth.

3 Spoon half the mixture into the prepared tin and smooth the surface with a palette knife. Arrange the peaches on top. Stir the cornflakes lightly into the remaining mixture, then drop spoonfuls of the mix over the peaches.

4 Bake in the preheated oven for about 1 hour, or until risen, firm and golden brown. Serve hot with whipped cream.

tropical fruit ring

ingredients

serves 12

oil or melted butter,
    for greasing
2 tbsp lime juice
100 g/3½ oz dried tropical fruit,
    such as mango, papaya
    and/or pineapple, roughly
    chopped, plus extra to decorate
175 g/6 oz plain white flour
2½ tsp baking powder
175 g/6 oz unsalted butter,
    softened
175 g/6 oz golden caster sugar
3 eggs, beaten
1 tsp vanilla extract

icing

70 g/2½ oz icing sugar
1 tbsp lime juice

method

1 Preheat the oven to 160°C/325°F/Gas Mark 3. Grease a
   1.5-litre/2¾-pint ring cake tin, preferably non-stick. Stir
   the lime juice into the dried tropical fruit and leave to
   soak for 15 minutes.

2 Sift the flour and baking powder into a large bowl and
   add the butter, caster sugar, eggs and vanilla extract.
   Beat well until the mixture is smooth, then stir in the
   soaked fruit.

3 Spoon the mixture into the prepared tin and smooth
   the surface with a palette knife. Bake in the preheated
   oven for 40–50 minutes, or until risen, firm and golden
   brown. Leave to cool in the tin for 10 minutes, then
   turn out and finish cooling on a wire rack.

4 For the icing, sift the icing sugar into a bowl, add the
   lime juice and stir until smooth. Spoon the icing over
   the cake and decorate with dried tropical fruit. Leave
   to set before slicing.

kiwi fruit cake with lemon frosting

ingredients

serves 8

oil or melted butter,
    for greasing
175 g/6 oz plain white flour
2 tsp baking powder
175 g/6 oz unsalted butter,
    softened
175 g/6 oz caster sugar
3 eggs, beaten
1 tsp vanilla extract
2 kiwi fruit, peeled and chopped
    into 1-cm/½-inch dice,
    plus extra slices to decorate

frosting

55 g/2 oz cream cheese
1 tbsp grated lemon rind
115 g/4 oz icing sugar

method

1 Preheat the oven to 160°C/325°F/Gas Mark 3. Grease and line a 1.2-litre/2-pint loaf tin.

2 Sift the flour and baking powder into a large bowl and add the butter, caster sugar, eggs and vanilla extract. Beat well until the mixture is smooth, then stir in half the chopped kiwi fruit.

3 Spoon the mixture into the prepared tin and smooth the surface with a palette knife. Scatter over the remaining chopped kiwi fruit. Bake in the preheated oven for about 1 hour, or until the cake is risen, firm and golden brown.

4 Leave to cool in the tin for 10 minutes, then turn out and finish cooling on a wire rack.

5 For the frosting, beat together the cream cheese, lemon rind and icing sugar until smooth. Spread the frosting over the cake and top with kiwi fruit slices.

citrus mousse cake

ingredients

serves 12

oil or melted butter,
    for greasing
175 g/6 oz butter
175 g/6 oz caster sugar
4 eggs, lightly beaten
200 g/7 oz self-raising flour
1 tbsp cocoa powder
50 g/1¾oz orange-flavoured
    plain chocolate, melted
peeled orange segments,
    to decorate

filling & topping

2 eggs, separated
50 g/1¾oz caster sugar
200 ml/7 fl oz freshly
    squeezed orange juice
2 tsp powdered gelatine
3 tbsp water
300 ml/10 fl oz double cream

method

1 Preheat the oven to 180°C/350°F/Gas Mark 4. Grease
   a 20-cm/8-inch round springform cake tin and line
   the base with baking paper.

2 Beat the butter and sugar in a bowl until light and
   fluffy. Gradually add the eggs, beating well after each
   addition. Sift together the flour and cocoa and fold into
   the creamed mixture. Fold in the melted chocolate.
   Pour into the prepared tin and smooth level. Bake in
   the preheated oven for about 40 minutes. Cool in the
   tin, then turn out onto a wire rack. Cut the cake
   horizontally and place the bottom half back in the tin.

3 For the filling, beat the egg yolks and sugar until pale,
   then whisk in the orange juice. Sprinkle the gelatine
   over the water in a small bowl and allow to go spongy,
   then place over a saucepan of hot water and stir until
   dissolved. Stir into the egg yolk mixture.

4 Whip the cream until holding its shape, reserve a little
   for the topping and fold the rest into the mousse.
   Whisk the egg whites until standing in soft peaks, then
   fold in. Leave in a cool place until starting to set, stirring
   occasionally. Pour the mixture into the tin and place
   the second half of the cake on top. Chill in the
   refrigerator until set. Turn out the cake, pipe cream
   around the top and decorate with orange segments.

lemon polenta cake

ingredients

serves 8

200 g/7 oz unsalted butter,
    plus extra for greasing
200 g/7 oz caster sugar
finely grated rind and juice of
    1 large lemon
3 eggs, beaten
140 g/5 oz ground almonds
100 g/3½ oz quick-cook polenta
1 tsp baking powder
crème fraîche, to serve

syrup

juice of 2 lemons
55 g/2 oz caster sugar
2 tbsp water

method

1 Preheat the oven to 180°C/350°F/Gas Mark 4. Lightly grease a 20-cm/8-inch round deep cake tin and line the base with baking paper.

2 Beat together the butter and sugar until pale and fluffy. Beat in the lemon rind, lemon juice, eggs and ground almonds. Sift in the polenta and baking powder and stir until evenly mixed.

3 Spoon the mixture into the prepared tin and spread evenly. Bake in the preheated oven for 30–35 minutes, or until just firm to the touch and golden brown. Remove the cake from the oven and leave to cool in the tin for 20 minutes.

4 For the syrup, place the lemon juice, sugar and water in a small saucepan. Heat gently, stirring until the sugar has dissolved, then bring to the boil and simmer for 3–4 minutes, or until slightly reduced and syrupy.

5 Turn out the cake onto a wire rack then drizzle half of the syrup evenly over the surface. Leave the cake to cool completely.

6 Cut the cake into slices, drizzle the extra syrup over the top and serve with crème fraîche.

orange & poppy seed bundt cake

ingredients
serves 10

200 g/7 oz unsalted butter,
     plus extra for greasing
200 g/7 oz golden caster sugar
3 large eggs, beaten
finely grated rind of 1 orange
55 g/2 oz poppy seeds
300 g/10½ oz plain flour,
     plus extra for dusting
2 tsp baking powder
150 ml/5 fl oz milk
125 ml/4 fl oz orange juice
strips of orange zest, to decorate

syrup
140 g/5 oz golden caster sugar
150 ml/5 fl oz orange juice

method

1 Preheat the oven to 160°C/325°F/Gas Mark 3. Grease and lightly flour a Bundt ring tin, about 24 cm/9 inches in diameter and with a capacity of approximately 2 litres/3½ pints.

2 Cream together the butter and sugar until pale and fluffy, then add the eggs gradually, beating thoroughly after each addition. Stir in the orange rind and poppy seeds. Sift in the flour and baking powder, then fold in evenly. Add the milk and orange juice, stirring to mix evenly.

3 Spoon the mixture into the prepared tin and bake in the preheated oven for 45–50 minutes, or until firm and golden brown. Leave to cool in the tin for 10 minutes, then turn out onto a wire rack to cool.

4 For the syrup, place the sugar and orange juice in a saucepan and heat gently until the sugar melts. Bring to the boil and simmer for about 5 minutes, until reduced and syrupy.

5 Spoon the syrup over the cake while it is still warm. Top with the strips of orange zest and serve warm or cold.

whole orange & almond cake

ingredients

serves 8–10

oil or melted butter,
    for greasing
2 oranges
55 g/2 oz ground almonds
115 g/4 oz plain white flour
1 tbsp baking powder
85 g/3 oz unsalted butter, softened
175 g/6 oz golden caster sugar
3 eggs, beaten
1 tsp orange flower water
2 tbsp orange juice
2 tbsp toasted flaked almonds
strips of orange zest,
    to decorate

method

1 Grease and line a 23-cm/9-inch round deep cake tin.

2 Wash the oranges and place in a saucepan, then cover with boiling water and simmer for 1 hour, covered, until soft. Drain and leave to cool slightly, then cut the oranges in half and remove and discard any pips. Purée in a food processor or blender until smooth, then stir in the ground almonds.

3 Preheat the oven to 160°C/325°F/Gas Mark 3. Sift the flour and baking powder into a large bowl and add the butter, sugar, eggs and orange flower water. Beat well until the mixture is smooth. Add the orange and almond mixture and the orange juice, mixing evenly.

4 Spoon the mixture into the prepared tin and smooth the surface with a palette knife. Bake in the preheated oven for 40–50 minutes, or until the cake is firm and golden brown.

5 Leave to cool in the tin for 2–3 minutes, then turn out and serve warm, topped with the flaked almonds and strips of orange zest.

clementine cake

ingredients

serves 8

175 g/6 oz butter, softened,
    plus extra for greasing
2 clementines
175 g/6 oz caster sugar
3 eggs, beaten
175 g/6 oz self-raising flour
3 tbsp ground almonds
3 tbsp single cream

glaze & topping

6 tbsp clementine juice
2 tbsp caster sugar
3 white sugar cubes, crushed

method

1 Preheat the oven to 180°C/350°F/Gas Mark 4. Grease an 18-cm/7-inch round cake tin with butter and line the base with baking paper.

2 Pare the rind from the clementines and chop the rind finely. In a bowl, cream together the butter, sugar and clementine rind until pale and fluffy.

3 Gradually add the beaten eggs to the mixture, beating thoroughly after each addition.

4 Gently fold in the self-raising flour followed by the ground almonds and the single cream. Spoon the mixture into the prepared tin.

5 Bake in the preheated oven for 55–60 minutes, or until a fine skewer inserted into the centre comes out clean. Leave in the tin to cool slightly.

6 Meanwhile, make the glaze. Put the clementine juice into a small saucepan with the caster sugar. Bring to the boil and simmer for 5 minutes.

7 Transfer the cake to a wire rack. Drizzle the glaze over the cake until it has been absorbed and sprinkle with the crushed sugar cubes.

mango & coconut brûlée cake

ingredients

serves 6

oil or melted butter,
    for greasing
1 large ripe mango, diced
175 g/6 oz plain white flour
1 tbsp baking powder
175 g/6 oz unsalted butter,
    softened
175 g/6 oz caster sugar
3 eggs, beaten
2 tbsp lime juice
finely grated rind of 1 lime
30 g/1 oz desiccated coconut
2 tbsp granulated sugar
toasted long-shred coconut,
    to decorate

method

1 Preheat the oven to 180°C/350°F/Gas Mark 4. Grease a 23-cm/9-inch round deep cake tin and line the base with baking paper.

2 Arrange the mango evenly over the base of the prepared tin. Sift the flour and baking powder into a large bowl and add the butter, caster sugar and eggs. Beat well until the mixture is smooth, then stir in the lime juice, lime rind and desiccated coconut.

3 Spoon the mixture over the mango and smooth the surface with a palette knife. Bake in the preheated oven for 40–50 minutes, or until the cake is risen, firm and golden brown.

4 Leave to cool in the tin for 2–3 minutes, then invert onto a flameproof dish. Preheat the grill to high. Sprinkle the top of the cake with granulated sugar and place under the hot grill for 2–3 minutes, until browned. Alternatively, use a chef's blowtorch to brown the top.

5 Serve hot, sprinkled with coconut shreds and cut into slices.

caramel apple upside-down cake

ingredients

serves 6

oil or melted butter,
    for greasing
175 g/6 oz plain white flour
1 tbsp baking powder
175 g/6 oz unsalted butter,
    softened
175 g/6 oz golden caster sugar
3 eggs, beaten
1 tsp vanilla extract
finely grated rind of 1 lemon

topping

55 g/2 oz unsalted butter
100 g/3½ oz caster sugar
1 tbsp water
4 eating apples
2 tbsp lemon juice

method

1 Preheat the oven to 180°C/350°F/Gas Mark 4. Grease a 23-cm/9-inch round deep cake tin with a solid base.

2 For the toffee apple topping, place the butter and sugar in a heavy-based saucepan with the water and heat gently until melted, then bring to the boil. Reduce the heat and cook, stirring, until it turns to a deep golden caramel colour. Pour quickly into the cake tin, tilting to cover the base evenly.

3 Peel, core and thickly slice the apples, toss with the lemon juice and spread evenly over the base of the cake tin.

4 Sift the flour and baking powder into a large bowl and add the butter, sugar, eggs and vanilla extract. Beat well until the mixture is smooth, then stir in the lemon rind.

5 Spoon the mixture over the apples and smooth the surface with a palette knife. Bake in the preheated oven for 40–50 minutes, or until risen and golden brown.

6 Leave to cool in the tin for 2–3 minutes, then turn out carefully onto a warmed serving plate.

spiced apple & sultana cake

ingredients

serves 8–10

225 g/8 oz unsalted butter,
softened, plus extra for
greasing
225 g/8 oz light muscovado sugar
4 large eggs, lightly beaten
225 g/ 8 oz self-raising flour
2 tsp ground cinnamon
½ tsp ground nutmeg
85 g/3 oz sultanas
3 small dessert apples, peeled,
cored and thinly sliced
2 tbsp clear honey, warmed

method

1 Preheat the oven to 180°C/350°F/Gas Mark 4. Grease
a 23-cm/9-inch round springform cake tin and line
the base with baking paper.

2 Place the butter and sugar in a large bowl and beat
together until light and fluffy. Gradually beat in the
eggs. Sift the flour, cinnamon and nutmeg into the
mixture and fold in gently using a metal spoon. Fold
in the sultanas.

3 Spoon half the mixture into the prepared tin and
level the surface. Scatter over half the sliced apples.
Spoon over the rest of the cake mixture and gently
level the surface. Arrange the rest of the apple slices
over the top of the cake.

4 Bake in the preheated oven for 1–1¼ hours until risen,
golden brown and firm to the touch. Leave to cool in
the tin for 10 minutes then turn out onto a wire rack.
Brush the top with the warmed honey and leave to
cool completely.

prune & armagnac cake

ingredients

serves 8

300 g/10½ oz ready-to-eat
    pitted prunes
150 ml/5 fl oz apple juice
3 tbsp armagnac or port
oil or melted butter,
    for greasing
175 g/6 oz plain white flour
2 tsp baking powder
175 g/6 oz unsalted butter,
    softened
175 g/6 oz light muscovado
    sugar
3 eggs, beaten
1 tsp vanilla extract
1 tbsp demerara sugar

method

1 Place the prunes in a pan with the apple juice and bring to the boil. Reduce the heat and simmer gently for 10 minutes, until the liquid is absorbed. Spoon over the armagnac and leave to cool completely.

2 Preheat the oven to 160°C/325°F/Gas Mark 4. Grease and line a 23-cm/9-inch round cake tin.

3 Sift the flour and baking powder into a large bowl and add the butter, muscovado sugar, eggs and vanilla extract. Beat well until the mixture is smooth.

4 Spoon the mixture into the prepared tin and smooth the surface with a palette knife. Drain the prunes well, reserving the juices, and arrange the prunes over the mixture in a single layer.

5 Bake in the preheated oven for 40–50 minutes, or until risen, firm and golden brown. Turn out onto a warmed serving plate with the prunes at the base and spoon over the reserved juices. Sprinkle with the demerara sugar and serve in slices.

glazed fruit & nut cake

ingredients

serves 16–18

oil or melted butter,
  for greasing
250 g/9 oz plain flour,
  plus extra for dusting
1 tbsp baking powder
1 tsp ground mixed spice
175 g/6 oz unsalted butter,
  softened
175 g/6 oz dark muscovado
  sugar
3 eggs, beaten
1 tsp vanilla extract
2 tbsp milk
300 g/10½ oz mixed dried fruit
85 g/3 oz chopped mixed nuts

topping

3 tbsp clear honey, warmed
350 g/12 oz mixed glacé
  fruits, such as pineapple,
  cherries and orange
55 g/2 oz whole shelled nuts,
  such as Brazil nuts,
  almonds and walnuts

method

1 Preheat the oven to 160°C/325°F/Gas Mark 3. Grease
  a 23-cm/9-inch round springform cake tin and sprinkle
  with a little flour to coat, shaking out the excess.

2 Sift the flour, baking powder and mixed spice into a
  large bowl and add the butter, sugar, eggs and vanilla
  extract. Beat well until the mixture is smooth, then stir
  in the milk, mixed dried fruit and chopped mixed nuts.

3 Spoon the mixture into the prepared tin and smooth
  level. Bake in the preheated oven for about 1 hour, or
  until risen, firm and golden brown.

4 Leave to cool in the tin for 30 minutes, then remove
  the sides and place on a wire rack to finish cooling.

5 Brush the top of the cake with a little of the warmed
  honey then arrange the glacé fruits and whole shelled
  nuts on top. Brush with the remaining honey and leave
  to set.

summer berry macaroons

ingredients

makes 6

75 g/2¾ oz ground almonds
115 g/4 oz icing sugar
2 large egg whites
50 g/1¾ oz caster sugar
fresh mint sprigs and whole
    strawberries, to decorate

filling

150 ml/5 fl oz double cream
2 tbsp lemon curd
115 g/4 oz small strawberries,
    hulled and quartered
115 g/4 oz raspberries
2 tbsp icing sugar

method

1 Place the ground almonds and icing sugar in a food processor and process for 15 seconds. Sift the mixture into a bowl. Line two baking sheets with baking paper.

2 Place the egg whites in a large bowl and whisk until holding soft peaks. Gradually whisk in the caster sugar to make a firm, glossy meringue. Using a spatula, fold the almond mixture into the meringue one third at a time. When all the dry ingredients are incorporated, continue to cut and fold the mixture until it forms a shiny batter with a thick, ribbon-like consistency.

3 Pour the mixture into a piping bag fitted with a 1-cm/ ½-inch plain nozzle. Pipe 12 large rounds onto the prepared baking sheets. Leave to stand for 30 minutes. Preheat the oven to 160°C/325°F/Gas Mark 3.

4 Bake in the preheated oven for 15–20 minutes. Cool for 10 minutes, then carefully peel the macaroons off the baking paper. Leave to cool completely.

5 For the filling, whip the cream until holding soft peaks, then fold in the lemon curd. Top half the macaroon shells with the lemon cream and two thirds of the berries. Purée the remaining berries with the icing sugar. Drizzle the purée over the berries and top with the remaining macaroons. Serve decorated with mint sprigs and whole strawberries.

blueberry cheesecake macaroons

ingredients

makes 16

75 g/2¼ oz ground almonds
115 g/4 oz icing sugar
2 large egg whites
50 g/1¾ oz caster sugar
½ tsp vanilla extract
blue food colouring paste
    or liquid

filling

115 g/4 oz soft cheese
2 tbsp soured cream
1 tbsp icing sugar
85 g/3 oz fresh blueberries,
    lightly crushed

method

1 Place the ground almonds and icing sugar in a food processor and process for 15 seconds. Sift the mixture into a bowl. Line two baking sheets with baking paper.

2 Place the egg whites in a large bowl and whisk until holding soft peaks. Gradually whisk in the caster sugar to make a firm, glossy meringue. Whisk in the vanilla extract and food colouring to give a bright blue colour.

3 Using a spatula, fold the almond mixture into the meringue one third at a time. When all the dry ingredients are thoroughly incorporated, continue to cut and fold the mixture until it forms a shiny batter with a thick, ribbon-like consistency.

4 Pour the mixture into a piping bag fitted with a 1-cm/½-inch plain nozzle. Pipe 32 small rounds onto the prepared baking sheets. Leave to stand for 30 minutes. Preheat the oven to 160°C/325°F/Gas Mark 3.

5 Bake in the preheated oven for 10–15 minutes. Cool for 10 minutes, then carefully peel the macaroons off the baking paper. Leave to cool completely.

6 For the filling, beat the soft cheese, soured cream and icing sugar together until smooth. Fold in the crushed blueberries. Use to sandwich pairs of macaroons together.

celebration cakes

birthday number cake

ingredients

serves 10–12

oil or melted butter,
    for greasing
175 g/6 oz plain white flour
1 tbsp baking powder
175 g/6 oz unsalted butter,
    softened
175 g/6 oz caster sugar
3 eggs, beaten
1 tsp vanilla extract
2 tbsp orange juice
finely grated rind of ½ orange
sugar orange slices and birthday
    candles, to decorate

topping

350 g/12 oz icing sugar, sifted
175 g/6 oz unsalted butter,
    softened
finely grated rind of ½ orange
1 tbsp orange juice

method

1 Preheat the oven to 160°C/325°F/Gas Mark 3. Grease and line a 25- x 18-cm/10- x 7-inch numeral cake tin or a frame on a baking sheet, about 5 cm/2 inches deep.

2 Sift the flour and baking powder into a large bowl and add the butter, caster sugar, eggs and vanilla extract. Beat well until the mixture is smooth, then stir in the orange juice and rind.

3 Spoon the mixture into the prepared tin and smooth the surface with a palette knife. Bake in the preheated oven for 40–50 minutes, or until risen, firm and golden brown. Leave to cool in the tin for 5 minutes, then turn out and finish cooling on a wire rack.

4 For the topping, beat together the icing sugar, butter, orange rind and juice until smooth. Spread over the cake evenly, smoothing with a palette knife.

5 Arrange the orange slices on top of the cake to decorate, then add the birthday candles and serve.

polka dot birthday cake

ingredients

serves 8–10

oil or melted butter,
  for greasing
175 g/6 oz plain white flour
1 tbsp baking powder
175 g/6 oz unsalted butter,
  softened
175 g/6 oz golden caster sugar
3 eggs, beaten
1 tsp vanilla extract
2 tbsp milk
coloured sweets and birthday
  candles, to decorate

filling & topping

5 tbsp apricot jam
1 tbsp lemon juice
500 g/1 lb 2 oz ready-to-roll
  soft icing

method

1 Preheat the oven to 160°C/325°F/Gas Mark 3. Grease and line two 20 cm/8-inch square sandwich tins.

2 Sift the flour and baking powder into a large bowl and add the butter, sugar, eggs and vanilla extract. Beat well until the mixture is smooth, then stir in the milk.

3 Divide the mixture between the prepared tins and smooth the surfaces with a palette knife. Bake in the preheated oven for 25–30 minutes, or until risen, firm and golden brown. Leave to cool in the tins for 2–3 minutes, then turn out and finish cooling on a wire rack.

4 Warm the apricot jam with the lemon juice in a small pan until melted. Spread half over one cake and place the other cake on top. Brush the remaining jam over the top and sides of the cakes.

5 Roll out the icing to cover the cakes, smoothing with your hands, then trim the edges with a sharp knife. Decorate with sweets and birthday candles.

mini cake pops

ingredients

makes 24

450 g/1 lb shop-bought sponge (vanilla or almond flavour)
85 g/3 oz mascarpone cheese
70 g/2½ oz icing sugar
½ tsp vanilla or almond extract
24 small coloured sweets and sugar sprinkles, to decorate

topping

225 g/8 oz milk chocolate, roughly chopped
24 lolly sticks
150 g/5½ oz fondant icing sugar
few drops of pink food colouring
4 tsp cold water

method

1 Line a baking tray with baking paper. Crumble the sponge cake into a mixing bowl. Add the mascarpone, icing sugar and vanilla and mix together until you have a thick paste.

2 Roll a 25 g/1 oz piece of the paste into a ball. Push this ball into a mini paper case, pressing it down so that when it is removed from the case you have a mini cupcake shape. Shape the remaining 23 cake pops in the same way. Place on the baking tray and chill in the refrigerator for 1–2 hours to firm up.

3 Put the chocolate in a heatproof bowl, set the bowl over a saucepan of gently simmering water and heat until melted. Remove from the heat. Push a lolly stick into each cake pop. Dip a cake pop into the chocolate, turning it until coated. Lift it from the bowl, letting the excess drip back into the bowl, then place it in a cup or tumbler. Repeat with the remaining cake pops. Chill or leave in a cool place until the chocolate has set.

4 Put the fondant icing sugar in a mixing bowl and beat in a dash of pink food colouring and the water until smooth. Spoon a little onto a cake pop, easing it slightly down the sides with a teaspoon. Before the icing sets, place a small sweet in the centre of each cake pop and scatter with sugar sprinkles.

tutti frutti whoopie pies

ingredients

makes 25

250 g/9 oz plain flour
1 tsp bicarbonate of soda
large pinch of salt
115 g/4 oz butter, softened
150 g/5½ oz caster sugar
1 large egg, beaten
½ tsp vanilla extract
150 ml/5 fl oz buttermilk
115 g/4 oz mixed coloured glacé
   cherries, finely chopped
4 tbsp multi-coloured sugar
   sprinkles

filling

225 g/8 oz white marshmallows
4 tbsp milk
few drops of red food colouring
115 g/4 oz white vegetable fat
55 g/2 oz icing sugar, sifted

method

1 Preheat the oven to 180°C/350°F/Gas Mark 4. Line 2–3 large baking sheets with baking paper. Sift together the plain flour, bicarbonate of soda and salt.

2 Place the butter and sugar in a large bowl and beat with an electric whisk until pale and fluffy. Beat in the egg and vanilla extract, half the flour mixture and buttermilk. Stir in the rest of the flour mixture and mix until incorporated. Stir in the chopped cherries.

3 Pipe or spoon 50 small mounds of the mixture onto the prepared baking sheets. Bake in the preheated oven, one sheet at a time, for 9–11 minutes, until risen and just firm to the touch. Cool for 5 minutes then transfer to a wire rack and leave to cool completely.

4 For the filling, place the marshmallows, milk and food colouring in a heatproof bowl set over a pan of simmering water. Let the marshmallows melt, stirring occasionally. Remove from the heat and leave to cool.

5 Place the white vegetable fat and icing sugar in a bowl and beat together until smooth and creamy. Add to the marshmallow and beat for 1–2 minutes until fluffy. To assemble, spread the filling over the flat side of half of the cakes. Top with the remaining cakes. Spread the sugar sprinkles on a plate and gently roll the edges of each whoopie pie in the sprinkles to lightly coat.

violet & lavender macaroons

ingredients

makes 16

75 g/2¾ oz ground almonds
115 g/4 oz icing sugar
2 large egg whites
50 g/1¾ oz lavender sugar
few drops of violet food colouring
1 tsp crystallized violets
1 tsp dried lavender

filling

115 g/4 oz soft cheese
2 tbsp lavender sugar

method

1 Place the ground almonds and icing sugar in a food processor and process for 15 seconds. Sift the mixture into a bowl. Line two baking sheets with baking paper.

2 Place the egg whites in a large bowl and whisk until holding soft peaks. Gradually whisk in the lavender sugar to make a firm, glossy meringue. Whisk in violet food colouring to give a pale violet colour.

3 Using a spatula, fold the almond mixture into the meringue one third at a time. When all the dry ingredients are incorporated, continue to cut and fold the mixture until it forms a shiny batter with a thick, ribbon-like consistency. Pour the mixture into a piping bag fitted with a 1-cm/½-inch plain nozzle. Pipe 32 small rounds onto the prepared baking sheets. Sprinkle over the crystallized violets and dried lavender. Leave at room temperature for 30 minutes. Preheat the oven to 160°C/325°F/Gas Mark 3.

4 Bake in the preheated oven for 10–15 minutes. Cool for 10 minutes, then carefully peel the macaroons off the baking paper. Leave to cool completely.

5 For the filling, beat together the soft cheese and lavender sugar until smooth. Use to sandwich pairs of macaroons together.

white chocolate valentine's gâteau

ingredients

serves 10

oil or melted butter,
    for greasing
175 g/6 oz plain white flour
1 tbsp baking powder
175 g/6 oz unsalted butter,
    softened
175 g/6 oz caster sugar
3 eggs, beaten
1 tsp vanilla extract
55 g/2 oz white chocolate, grated
2 tbsp white rum (optional)
crystallized violets, to decorate

frosting

200 g/7 oz white chocolate,
    broken into pieces
2 tbsp milk
200 ml/7 fl oz double cream

method

1 Preheat the oven to 160°C/325°F/Gas Mark 3. Grease a 1.5-litre/2¾-pint heart-shaped cake tin.

2 Sift the flour and baking powder into a bowl and add the butter, sugar, eggs and vanilla extract. Beat well until smooth, then stir in the grated chocolate.

3 Spoon the mixture into the prepared tin and smooth the surface with a palette knife. Bake in the preheated oven for 45–55 minutes, or until risen, firm and golden brown. Leave to cool in the tin for 10 minutes, then turn out onto a wire rack to finish cooling.

4 For the frosting, melt the chocolate with the milk in a heatproof bowl set over a pan of hot water. Remove from the heat and stir until smooth, then leave to cool for 10 minutes. Whip the cream until it holds soft peaks, then fold into the cooled chocolate mixture.

5 Sprinkle the cake with the rum, if using. Spread the frosting over the top and sides of the cake, swirling with a palette knife, then decorate the cake with crystallized violets.

valentine chocolate heart cake

ingredients

serves 12

175 g/6 oz self-raising flour
2 tsp baking powder
55 g/2 oz cocoa powder
3 eggs
140 g/5 oz light muscovado sugar
150 ml/5 fl oz sunflower oil,
    plus extra for greasing
150 ml/5 fl oz single cream
fresh mint sprigs, to decorate

filling & topping

225 g/8 oz plain chocolate,
    broken into pieces
250 ml/9 fl oz double cream
200 g/7 oz fresh or frozen
    raspberries
3 tbsp seedless raspberry jam

method

1 Preheat the oven to 180°C/350°F/Gas Mark 4. Grease a 20-cm/8-inch heart-shaped tin and line the base with baking paper.

2 Sift the flour, baking powder and cocoa powder into a large bowl. Beat the eggs with the sugar, oil and single cream. Make a well in the dry ingredients and add the egg mixture, then stir to mix thoroughly, beating to a smooth batter.

3 Pour the mixture into the prepared tin and bake in the preheated oven for 25–30 minutes, or until risen and firm to the touch. Leave to cool in the tin, then turn out and finish cooling on a wire rack.

4 For the filling and topping, place the chocolate and double cream in a saucepan over a low heat and stir until melted. Remove from the heat and stir until the mixture cools slightly and begins to thicken.

5 Use a sharp knife to cut the cake in half horizontally. Spread the cut surface of each half with the raspberry jam, then top with about 3 tablespoons of the chocolate mixture. Scatter half the raspberries over the base and replace the top, pressing lightly. Spread the remaining chocolate mixture over the top and sides of the cake, swirling with a palette knife. Top with the remaining raspberries and decorate with mint sprigs.

traditional simnel cake

ingredients

serves 16

175 g/6 oz unsalted butter,
  plus extra for greasing
175 g/6 oz light muscovado sugar
3 eggs, beaten
225 g/8 oz plain flour
½ tsp baking powder
2 tsp ground mixed spice
finely grated rind of 1 small lemon
100 g/3½ oz currants
100 g/3½ oz sultanas
55 g/2 oz chopped mixed peel

topping

700 g/1 lb 9 oz marzipan
3 tbsp apricot jam

method

1 Preheat the oven to 150°C/300°F/Gas Mark 2. Grease and line a 20-cm/8-inch round deep cake tin with baking paper.

2 Place the butter and sugar in a bowl and cream together with an electric whisk until pale, light and fluffy. Gradually beat in the eggs. Sift together the flour, baking powder and mixed spice and fold into the creamed mixture. Stir in the lemon rind, currants, sultanas and mixed peel, mixing evenly. Spoon half the mixture into the prepared tin and smooth level.

3 Roll out 250 g/9 oz of the marzipan to a 20-cm/8-inch round and place over the mixture in the tin. Add the remaining cake mixture and smooth level. Bake the cake in the preheated oven for 2¼–2¾ hours, or until firm and golden. Leave to cool in the tin for 30 minutes, then turn out onto a wire rack to finish cooling.

4 Brush the top of the cake with apricot jam. Roll out two thirds of the remaining marzipan to a round to cover the top of the cake. Use a knife to mark a lattice design in the surface and pinch the edges to decorate.

5 Roll the remaining marzipan into 11 small balls and decorate the edge of the cake. Place under a hot grill for 30–40 seconds to brown lightly. Cool before serving.

easter cupcakes

ingredients

serves 16

115 g/4 oz butter, softened
115 g/4 oz caster sugar
2 eggs, lightly beaten
85 g/3 oz self-raising flour
25 g/1 oz cocoa powder
    for the topping
85 g/3 oz butter, softened
175 g/6 oz icing sugar
1 tbsp milk
2–3 drops of vanilla extract
2 x 130 g/4½ oz packets
    mini chocolate candy
    shell eggs

method

1 Preheat the oven to 180°C/350°F/Gas Mark 4. Put 12 paper cases on a bun tray or put 12 double-layer paper cases on a baking tray.

2 Put the butter and sugar in a bowl and beat together until light and fluffy. Gradually add the eggs, beating well after each addition. Sift in the flour and cocoa powder and, using a large metal spoon, fold into the mixture. Spoon the mixture into the paper cases.

3 Bake the cupcakes in the preheated oven for 15–20 minutes, or until well risen and firm to the touch. Transfer to a wire rack and leave to cool.

4 For the butter-cream topping, put the butter in a bowl. Sift in the icing sugar and beat together until well mixed, adding the milk and vanilla extract.

5 When the cupcakes are cold, put the icing in a piping bag, fitted with a large star nozzle, and pipe a circle around the edge of each cupcake to form a nest. Place chocolate eggs in the centre of each nest, to decorate. Serve.

silver wedding anniversary cake

ingredients

serves 10–12

oil or melted butter,
    for greasing
175 g/6 oz plain white flour
1 tbsp baking powder
175 g/6 oz unsalted butter,
    softened
175 g/6 oz caster sugar
3 eggs, beaten
1 tsp vanilla extract
2 tbsp milk
2 tbsp medium sherry
silver dragées, to decorate

frosting

250 g/9 oz mascarpone cheese
3 tbsp single cream
500 g/1 lb 2 oz icing sugar, sifted,
    plus extra if needed

method

1 Preheat the oven to 180°C/350°F/Gas Mark 4. Grease an 18-cm/7-inch sandwich tin and a 23-cm/9-inch sandwich tin and line the bases with baking paper.

2 Sift the flour and baking powder into a large bowl and add the butter, caster sugar, eggs and vanilla extract. Beat well until the mixture is smooth, then stir in the milk.

3 Spoon the mixture into the prepared tins and smooth the surfaces with a palette knife. Bake in the preheated oven for 20–25 minutes for the small cake and 25–30 minutes for the large cake, or until risen, firm and golden brown.

4 Leave to cool in the tins for 2–3 minutes, then turn out and finish cooling on wire racks. Prick the cakes with a skewer and sprinkle with the sherry.

5 For the frosting, beat together the mascarpone, cream and icing sugar to a smooth, spreading consistency, adding a little more icing sugar if needed. Spread a little frosting on top of the centre of the larger cake, then place the small cake on top, pressing down lightly.

6 Spread the remaining frosting over the cakes, swirling with a palette knife, then decorate with silver dragées before serving.

rose gâteau

ingredients

serves 8–10

oil or melted butter,
    for greasing
175 g/6 oz plain white flour
1 tbsp baking powder
175 g/6 oz unsalted butter,
    softened
175 g/6 oz caster sugar
3 eggs, beaten
1 tsp rosewater
2 tbsp milk

filling & icing

150 ml/5 fl oz whipping cream
1 tsp rosewater
200 g/7 oz icing sugar, sifted

decoration

fresh rose petals, washed
    and patted dry
½ egg white
caster sugar, for sprinkling

method

1 Preheat the oven to 180°C/350°F/Gas Mark 4. Grease two 23-cm/9-inch sandwich tins and line the bases with baking paper.

2 Sift the flour and baking powder into a large bowl and add the butter, caster sugar, eggs and rosewater. Beat well until the mixture is smooth, then stir in the milk.

3 Divide the mixture between the prepared tins and smooth the surfaces with a palette knife. Bake in the preheated oven for 25–30 minutes, or until risen, firm and golden brown. Leave to cool in the tins for 2–3 minutes, then turn out and finish cooling on a wire rack.

4 Whip the cream with ½ teaspoon of the rosewater until just thick enough to hold its shape. Use to sandwich the cakes together.

5 For the icing, mix the icing sugar with the remaining rosewater and just enough water to mix to a thick pouring consistency. Spoon over the cake, allowing it to drizzle down the sides. Leave to set.

6 Brush the rose petals with the egg white, sprinkle with caster sugar and arrange on top of the cake.

halloween pumpkin cake

ingredients

serves 10

oil or melted butter,
    for greasing
175 g/6 oz plain white flour
1 tbsp baking powder
1 tsp ground mixed spice
175 g/6 oz unsalted butter,
    softened
175 g/6 oz light muscovado
    sugar
3 eggs, beaten
1 tsp vanilla extract
175 g/6 oz pumpkin flesh,
    coarsely grated

topping

3 tbsp apricot jam, warmed
a few drops of orange and black
    food colouring
800 g/1 lb 12 oz ready-to-roll
    soft icing
black, green and yellow
    writing icing

method

1 Preheat the oven to 160°C/325°F/Gas Mark 3. Grease and line a 23-cm/9-inch round deep cake tin.

2 Sift the flour, baking powder and mixed spice into a bowl and add the butter, sugar, eggs and vanilla extract. Beat well until smooth, then stir in the grated pumpkin.

3 Spoon the mixture into the prepared tin and spread the top level. Bake in the preheated oven for 40–50 minutes, or until risen, firm and golden brown. Leave to cool in the tin for 10 minutes, then turn out onto a wire rack to finish cooling.

4 Brush the cake with warmed apricot jam. Knead orange food colouring into about three quarters of the icing and roll out to cover the top and sides of the cake. Trim the edges neatly, reserving the trimmings.

5 Form the trimmings into small pumpkin shapes and use the black writing icing to pipe faces and the green writing icing to pipe stalks onto them. Knead black food colouring into the remaining icing, then roll it out and cut into bat shapes. Pipe eyes onto the bats using yellow writing icing, then place the bats and the pumpkins onto the cake to decorate.

halloween spider's web cake

ingredients

serves 8–10

115 g/4 oz unsalted butter,
    plus extra for greasing
115 g/4 oz caster sugar
2 eggs, beaten
3 tbsp milk
140 g/5 oz self-raising flour
½ tsp baking powder
a few drops of orange food
    colouring

topping

2 tbsp apricot jam, warmed
500 g/1 lb 2 oz ready-to-roll icing
    (three quarters coloured
    orange and one quarter black),
    plus extra black food colouring
100 g/3½ oz icing sugar,
    plus extra for dusting

method

1 Preheat the oven to 160°C/325°F/Gas Mark 3. Grease an 18-cm/7-inch round cake tin and line the base with baking paper.

2 Cream together the butter and caster sugar until light and fluffy. Beat in the eggs and milk. Sift in the flour and baking powder, then fold in. Spoon half the mixture into a separate bowl and stir in a few drops of orange food colouring. Place alternate spoonfuls of the plain and orange mixtures into the prepared cake tin, swirling lightly for a marbled effect. Bake in the preheated oven for 35–40 minutes. Leave to cool, then turn out and finish cooling on a wire rack.

3 Place the cake on a plate and brush the top and sides with apricot jam. Roll out the orange icing on a surface lightly dusted with icing sugar, then lift it onto the cake. Trim the edges, reserving the trimmings.

4 Place the icing sugar in a bowl and stir in enough water to mix to a paste, adding a few drops of black food colouring. Spoon into a small piping bag fitted with a medium plain nozzle, then pipe a spider's web design over the top of the cake. Shape about half of the black icing into an oval for the spider's body, then shape eight legs from the black icing. Shape two eyes from the orange icing trimmings. Place on the web.

pina colada whoopie pies

ingredients

makes 12

225 g/8 oz plain flour

2 tsp baking powder

large pinch of salt

55 g/2 oz desiccated coconut

115 g/4 oz butter, softened

150 g/5½ oz caster sugar

1 large egg, beaten

100 ml/3½ fl oz milk

25 g/1 oz crystallized pineapple, finely chopped

toasted coconut shavings, to decorate

filling

300 ml/10 fl oz double cream

2 tbsp white rum

icing

115 g/4 oz icing sugar

1–2 tbsp pineapple juice

method

1 Preheat the oven to 180°C/350°F/Gas Mark 4. Line 2–3 large baking sheets with baking paper. Sift together the plain flour, baking powder and salt. Stir in the coconut.

2 Place the butter and sugar in a large bowl and beat with an electric whisk until pale and fluffy. Beat in the egg followed by half the flour mixture then the milk. Stir in the rest of the flour mixture and mix until incorporated. Fold in the chopped pineapple.

3 Pipe or spoon 24 mounds of the mixture onto the prepared baking sheets, spaced well apart to allow for spreading. Bake in the preheated oven, one sheet at a time, for 10–12 minutes until risen and just firm to the touch. Cool for 5 minutes then using a palette knife transfer to a wire rack and leave to cool completely.

4 For the filling, place the cream and rum in a bowl and whip together until holding firm peaks. For the icing, sift the icing sugar into a bowl and gradually stir in enough pineapple juice to make a smooth icing.

5 To assemble, spread or pipe the rum cream on the flat side of half the cakes. Top with the rest of the cakes. Spoon the icing over the whoopie pies letting it drip down the sides. Decorate with toasted coconut shavings. Leave to set.

christmas macaroons

ingredients

makes 16

75 g/2¾ oz ground almonds
115 g/4 oz icing sugar
1 tsp ground mixed spice
2 large egg whites
50 g/1¾ oz golden caster sugar
½ tsp freshly grated nutmeg
1 tsp gold or silver dragées

filling

55 g/2 oz unsalted butter,
    softened
finely grated rind and juice
    of ½ orange
1 tsp ground mixed spice
115 g/4 oz icing sugar, sifted
25 g/1 oz glacé cherries,
    finely chopped

method

1 Place the ground almonds, icing sugar and mixed spice in a food processor and process for 15 seconds. Sift the mixture into a bowl. Line two baking sheets with baking paper.

2 Place the egg whites in a large bowl and whisk until holding soft peaks. Gradually whisk in the caster sugar to make a firm, glossy meringue. Using a spatula, fold the almond mixture into the meringue one third at a time. When all the dry ingredients are incorporated, continue to cut and fold the mixture until it forms a shiny batter with a thick, ribbon-like consistency.

3 Pour the mixture into a piping bag fitted with a 1-cm/½-inch plain nozzle. Pipe 32 small rounds onto the prepared baking sheets. Sprinkle half the macaroons with the grated nutmeg and dragées. Leave for 30 minutes. Preheat the oven to 160°C/325°F/Gas Mark 3. Bake in the preheated oven for 10–15 minutes. Cool for 10 minutes, then peel the macaroons off the baking paper. Leave to cool completely.

4 For the filling, beat the butter and orange rind and juice in a bowl until fluffy. Gradually beat in the mixed spice and icing sugar until smooth and creamy. Fold in the glacé cherries. Use to sandwich pairs of macaroons together.

golden christmas cake

ingredients

serves 16–18

175 g/6 oz dried apricots, chopped

85 g/3 oz dried mango, chopped

85 g/3 oz dried pineapple, chopped

175 g/6 oz sultanas

55 g/2 oz chopped stem ginger

55 g/2 oz chopped mixed peel

finely grated rind and juice of 1 orange

4 tbsp brandy

oil or melted butter, for greasing

175 g/6 oz unsalted butter

100 g/3½ oz light muscovado sugar

4 eggs, beaten

2 tbsp clear honey

175 g/6 oz self-raising flour

2 tsp ground allspice

85 g/3 oz pecan nuts

silver dragées, to decorate

topping

800 g/1 lb 12 oz marzipan

900 g/2 lb ready-to-roll icing

method

1 Place the chopped apricots, mango and pineapple in a bowl with the sultanas, stem ginger and mixed peel. Stir in the orange rind, orange juice and brandy. Cover the bowl and leave to soak overnight.

2 Preheat the oven to 160°C/325°F/Gas Mark 3. Grease a 23-cm/9-inch round springform cake tin and line with baking paper.

3 Cream together the butter and sugar until the mixture is pale and fluffy. Add the eggs to the mixture, beating well between each addition. Stir in the honey. Sift the flour with the allspice and fold into the mixture using a metal spoon. Add the soaked fruit and pecan nuts, stirring thoroughly to mix. Spoon the mixture into the prepared tin, spreading evenly, then make a slight dip in the centre.

4 Place the tin in the centre of the preheated oven and bake for 1½–2 hours, or until golden brown and firm to the touch and a skewer inserted into the centre comes out clean. Leave to cool in the tin.

5 Turn the cake out, remove the lining paper and re-wrap in clean baking paper and foil. Store in a cool place for at least 1 month before use. Cover the cake with marzipan and ready-to-roll icing, following the pack instructions, and decorate with silver dragées.

christmas mulled sponge loaf

ingredients

serves 8

oil or melted butter,
   for greasing
175 g/6 oz plain flour
1 tbsp baking powder
1 tsp ground mixed spice
175 g/6 oz unsalted butter,
   softened
175 g/6 oz light muscovado
   sugar
3 eggs, beaten
1 tsp vanilla extract
finely grated rind of 1 orange
2 tbsp orange juice

syrup

70 g/2½ oz icing sugar
100 ml/3½ fl oz port or
   red wine
1 piece star anise

decoration

10 fresh cranberries
10 fresh bay leaves
1 egg white
caster sugar, for sprinkling

method

1 Preheat the oven to 180°C/350°F/Gas Mark 4. Grease a 1.2-litre/2-pint loaf tin and line with baking paper.

2 Sift the flour, baking powder and mixed spice into a large bowl and add the butter, muscovado sugar, eggs and vanilla extract. Beat well until the mixture is smooth, then stir in the orange rind and juice.

3 Spoon the mixture into the prepared tin and smooth level. Bake in the preheated oven for 40–50 minutes, or until risen, firm and golden brown. (Don't worry if the cake dips slightly in the centre.)

4 Remove the tin from the oven and stand it on a wire rack. To make the syrup, place the icing sugar, port and star anise in a pan and heat gently until boiling. Boil rapidly for 2–3 minutes to reduce slightly. Remove and discard the star anise.

5 Spoon the syrup over the cake and leave to soak for 30 minutes. Turn out the cake from the tin, so it is upside down.

6 Brush the cranberries and bay leaves with egg white and sprinkle with caster sugar, then arrange on top of the cake.

snowflake whoopie pies

ingredients

makes 14

200 g/7 oz plain flour
2 tsp baking powder
large pinch of salt
55 g/2 oz ground almonds
115 g/4 oz butter, softened
150 g/5½ oz caster sugar,
    plus extra for sprinkling
1 large egg, beaten
1 tsp almond extract
100 ml/3½ fl oz milk
1 tbsp silver dragées

filling

150 g/5½ oz unsalted butter,
    softened
8 tbsp double cream
280 g/10 oz icing sugar, sifted

icing

115 g/4 oz icing sugar
1–2 tbsp warm water

method

1 Preheat the oven to 180°C/350°F/Gas Mark 4. Line 2–3 large baking sheets with baking paper. Sift together the plain flour, baking powder and salt. Stir in the ground almonds. Place the butter and sugar in a large bowl and beat with an electric whisk until pale and fluffy. Beat in the egg and almond extract followed by half the flour mixture then the milk. Stir in the rest of the flour mixture and beat until thoroughly incorporated.

2 Pipe or spoon 28 mounds of the mixture onto the prepared baking sheets. Bake in the preheated oven, one sheet at a time, for 10–12 minutes until risen and just firm to the touch. Cool, then transfer to a wire rack and leave to cool completely.

3 For the filling, place the butter in a bowl and beat with an electric whisk for 2–3 minutes until pale and creamy. Beat in the cream then gradually beat in the icing sugar until light and fluffy. For the icing, sift the icing sugar into a bowl and gradually stir in enough water to make a smooth, thick icing.

4 To assemble, spread or pipe the buttercream on the flat side of half of the cakes. Top with the rest of the cakes. Spoon the icing into a small paper piping bag, snip the end and pipe snowflake patterns. Decorate with silver dragées and sprinkle with caster sugar. Leave to set.

index